# Seasonal Pleasures

## RECIPES FROM A FARMHOUSE KITCHEN

## ROSAMOND RICHARDSON

*Illustrated by Julie Banyard*

VIKING

*Dedicated to my grandfather,*

*who died in 1982 at the age of one hundred years*

**VIKING**

Published by the Penguin Group
27 Wrights Lane, London W8 5TZ, England
Viking Penguin Inc., 40 West 23rd Street, New York, New York 10010, USA
Penguin Books Australia Ltd, Ringwood, Victoria, Australia
Penguin Books Canada Ltd, 2801 John Street, Markham, Ontario, Canada L3R 1B4
Penguin Books (NZ) Ltd, 182–190 Wairau Road, Auckland 10, New Zealand

Penguin Books Ltd, Registered Offices: Harmondsworth, Middlesex, England

First published 1990

1 3 5 7 9 10 8 6 4 2

Copyright © Rosamund Richardson, 1990
Illustrations copyright © Julie Banyard, 1990

The acknowledgements on p. 156 constitute an extension of this copyright page.

Filmset in Sabon by Wyvern Typesetting Ltd, Bristol
Printed in Italy

A CIP catalogue record for this book is available from the British Library

ISBN 0–670–82052–0

# Contents

# Introduction

This book is a personal anthology. It is also a recipe book, but one that embraces the English countryside, the seasons, folklore and festivals, favourite poems and pieces of prose, along with food. I wrote it in my cottage in a small country village as the year turned, gathering all the strands together through the changing seasons, tasting all the dishes as their ingredients ripened or came on to the market, thinking about the book as I walked the country lanes. I need hardly say that it has been a treat to work on – if this is a job, it feels more like a luxury!

My interest in nature and folklore goes back to childhood, which was a city childhood. I always longed to live in the country, and, because I didn't, I lived there in my imagination. It was only years later, when I came to know my grandfather well, that I realized I had inherited this love from him – it had skipped a generation. This book is lovingly dedicated to his memory.

As a child, the garden we had in Cambridge was my paradise, and, to some extent, it made up for not living in the depths of the countryside – for a while, anyway. I remember long grass under the apple trees late on summer evenings; so tall it seemed, as I lay hidden, inhaling its damp sweetness. I remember the colourful herbaceous border carefully tended by my mother; the old quince tree that leaned dangerously over the bank and under which, every spring, grew scillas and chionodoxa. The old 'ivy tree', as we called it (an ancient, hollow tree-trunk, elm I think, covered in tangled ivy), was a refuge from what appeared to me the insanities and trials of life. I gazed at daffodils in wonder, and marvelled at the bright blueness of periwinkle clambering in the hedge.

It was not until much later in life that I moved into a country cottage, and, when I did, it was as if a dream had come true and I had come home. 'The country habit has me by the heart', as Vita Sackville-West puts it: the changing seasons, fields and hedgerows, the clean night air, wild flowers in spring, never fail to enchant – indeed, every year my awareness of them seems to sharpen. I love walking in all weathers, hearing the first spring birds or watching a late sun sink over cornfields in summer. Watching a lark hovering over her nest in the wheat, hearing the roar of the combine at harvest, feeling a bitter north wind bring the first of the winter sleet.

At last, happily working in a cottage kitchen, I have put together a collection of recipes that follow the turning year. They are as English as cookery can be at a time of enormous change: supermarkets have undergone a revolution in the past few years and have affected our shopping patterns, our eating habits, the way we cook and our approach to food. The supermarket shelves in my local town are laden with exotic and unusual produce from all over the world, and provide me with fresh herbs, rare spices and unheard-of fish throughout the year. This book reflects these changes simply because it has been written at this time. Nevertheless, I treasure our heritage of traditional English dishes, and have included many, particularly in the festive recipe chapters.

Cookery writers from all corners of the globe have recently published numerous books, apparently eager to share their culinary art, and I have also experimented with these different cookery cultures. On the way I became interested in the trend for healthy eating, so there are no recipes for meat included in this book, although there are some for fish. Being an artist by training, I am interested in how things look, and have paid some attention to the details of garnishes and colours of the dishes.

Food as an art form fascinates me: it can look beautiful, taste exquisite, smell wonderful, make people feel good, bring them together, inspire romantic feelings, help them to share things. At its most basic, it is fuel for a hungry machine; it satisfies the appetite, provides energy and helps the body to grow and to stay healthy. Of course, eating *can* be a bad experience, but with any luck not all that often: at its best, food is life-enhancing, and that is the viewpoint I have adopted as part of my personal philosophy.

I was brought up in very literary surroundings: my father was a scholar, and the walls of our house were lined with books. There was no television and I didn't know how to work the radio (in any case, it was kept high up on a shelf, out of reach of little fingers), so I was usually to be found curled up with my nose in a book – either in that long grass or up the quince tree if it was warm enough to be outside. It has therefore been pure pleasure selecting some of my favourite poems and pieces of prose to weave into the text. Their inclusion turns what might on first appearance look like a cookery book into a bedside book, as well as a practical book for the kitchen. Well, why not? Many of my friends tell me that they take recipe books to bed with them!

The cottage I live in now looks out over a quiet village street in East Anglia, where the road turns towards fields farmed mostly for wheat and barley. I sit by the kitchen window listening to the stream running under the bridge, and to spring birds cheeping in the chestnut tree by the corner of the thatch. A distant dog barks. One of my neighbours cycles past on his weekly visit to the post office to collect his pension. A little later a woman walks her dog along the path and across a field, up towards the wood. I am content in my cottage kitchen – by no means everyone's ideal of a working kitchen because it is so small, but I make the most of modern gadgets and have no complaints. It means that I make cooking as simple as possible – a characteristic of the recipes in this book – for just that reason! The mouth-watering smell of ginger and garlic from the Chinese dish I have just tried out for the book still lingers: it reminds me that it is time to eat. All I need is a few herbs for the salad.

The garden here is small and very pretty. It is surrounded by thick hedges; to one side of the lawn stands an old Bramley apple tree, giving welcome shade on hot days. The rockery at the top of the garden is full of colourful, delicate alpine flowers in summer, and down one side of the lawn runs a border that is crowded with cottage plants and old roses. I have planted them everywhere possible – climbers, ramblers, shrubs – so that at midsummer I am surrounded by the old-fashioned roses that I love so much.

I made a tiny formal herb garden soon after I came, with a brick path down the middle and a stone bird-bath as its focal point. I love herbs; they have a magic and a special beauty that I do not like to live without. In spring, when they are all in flower, the herb garden is a picture, and I inhale the delicate scents as I pick them, judiciously, for the day's salad. I will do the same in spring and summer: sage, lovage, tarragon, parsley, rosemary, thyme and fennel are all indispensable to summery meals. I have discovered that their folklore and history are fascinating, too, and have collected many old books on herbs, including some herbals, for my library.

It will have become clear that this book is a very personal one. In it are gathered many of the things that give me the greatest pleasure through the seasons, year after year, and of which I never tire. My hope is that by inviting you, the reader, into my cottage kitchen to share the delights of contemporary English cooking, along with the pleasures of the countryside and a poem or two, you will find as much pleasure in them as I do.

*Rosamond Richardson*

*Summer*

# Summer

# Raw Food

# Seasonal Side Vegetables

# Light Fruit Desserts

# The Picnic Basket

Horses, their heads together under a tree;
Elm-trees and oaks, mantled in glistening green;
Streams silver-brimmed, the stream-divided lea,
Wide-rising ground with barley thronged or bean:
A town-end of good houses, something grave,
Gray, square, and windowing far; cypress and yew
Topping a long gray wall; five poplars wave
Above the dark-plumed wall; against high blue
Spear-flashing white the spire, and windcock new
Aloft the spire, proud plaything of these gales
Which bring more violet wreaths of cloud and swirl
Of whistling rain; the storm's great ghost assails
The boys with bat and ball, the blue-capped girl
Who leans with her young love against the pales;
While over the level the terrier speeds and springs,
Hoping to catch the swallows in their low swift rings.

Edmund Blunden, *Village Sketch*

# Mushroom and Parsley Pâté

SERVES 4–6

I love picnics – that is, picnics with style. I am not a sandwich-and-thermos person when it comes to it, because our fine summer days are rare, rare enough to merit the creation of something special. So I start this section with a delectable mushroom pâté, light and creamy in texture and with a delicacy of flavour that gets any picnic off to a great start.

Cook the mushrooms and the spring onions in the butter or margarine until well softened down (about 7–8 minutes). Stir in the breadcrumbs and mix well. Put this mixture into the food processor with the garlic, lemon juice and curd cheese, and blend to a smooth purée. Mix in the chopped parsley and season to taste. Place in a container and chill until ready to pack into the picnic basket. Try serving it with wholemeal pitta bread – they are excellent together.

250 g (8 oz) mushrooms, chopped

6 spring onions, finely sliced

50 g (2 oz) butter or margarine

2 tbls fresh wholemeal breadcrumbs

1 large clove of garlic, crushed

2 tsp lemon juice

125 g (4 oz) low-fat curd cheese

1 medium bunch of parsley, finely chopped

ground nutmeg to taste

salt and pepper

## Dill Herrings

SERVES 4

A far cry from the average rollmop, these aromatic herrings make a delicious addition to a picnic lunch. The dill gives them a truly summery flavour, and little dice of cucumber make a perfect balance to the fish itself. The great advantage of this recipe is that you can prepare it several days in advance if you like.

Cut the fish into 4 strips lengthwise and then cut each strip in half. Sprinkle the dill and onion over the top, and put into a large glass jar with a screw-top lid. Combine the remaining ingredients and pour over the fish. Marinate for at least 12 hours. The jar can be stored in the refrigerator for up to a week.

2 herrings, filleted

3 tbls dill, chopped

1 small onion, chopped

half a cucumber, peeled and diced

300 ml ($\frac{1}{2}$ pt) white wine vinegar

1 tbls salt

1 tbls sugar

## Greek Stuffed Tomatoes

SERVES 6

These are sensational. Greece is probably my favourite country abroad, and I need more than occasional reminders of its smells and tastes and atmosphere. The aroma of thyme, the taste of crumbly feta cheese, sun-ripe tomatoes and a touch of tahini all help to conjure up the brilliant blue skies, turquoise seas and mist-blue mountains that I love.

Scoop the seeds and flesh out of the tomatoes and turn upside down to drain thoroughly. Combine the feta with the olive oil, herbs and spring onions. Mix the tahini into the mayonnaise and blend thoroughly. Add to the cheese mixture and stir together well. Pile into the tomato shells and chill. These are delicious served with a bowl of black olives to hand around.

3 large beef tomatoes, cut in half

125 g (4 oz) feta cheese, finely crumbled

2 tbls Greek olive oil

2 tbls thyme and oregano, chopped

1 tbls coriander, chopped

4 spring onions, very finely sliced

2 tsp tahini

5 tbls mayonnaise (see p. 148)

# Cold Omelette Roll Provençale

SERVES 4

Another party-piece: an original addition to a picnic basket with fresh, summery tastes and mouth-watering texture. These omelette rolls take a little while to prepare, but they are really worth the work. They look lovely, too, and make delicious mouthfuls on pieces of fresh wholemeal bread. Have them with a bottle of light red wine (if no one did the classic thing of leaving the corkscrew behind...).

Cook the garlic and onion in the olive oil over a medium heat for 5 minutes. Add the chopped tomatoes and herbs, and cook gently for a further 10 minutes, until everything is well softened and amalgamated. Season to taste, and leave to cool, covered.

Mix the milk into the beaten eggs and season to taste. Make four very fine, thin omelettes in the usual way, using a heavy pan and a little butter. Put each one out flat to cool. Cover their surfaces with a quarter of the Provençale filling, roll up and chill. Cut into 1-cm ($\frac{1}{2}$-in) slices, wrap securely in cling-film, and then pack into a plastic box for the hamper.

1 clove of garlic, finely chopped

1 small onion, finely chopped

2 tbls olive oil

2 large tomatoes, peeled and chopped

8 sprigs of parsley, finely chopped

2 sprigs of tarragon, finely chopped

salt and pepper

4 tbls milk

4 eggs, beaten

salt and pepper

a little butter

*What is success in life? To laugh often and much, to win the affection of children, to find the best in others, to endure the betrayal of false friends, to make the world a better place to live in than when we were born into it, by rearing a little garden patch, improving some social condition, or helping a child to grow healthier. To know that one life breathes easier since you lived. That is success.*

Emerson

# Pasta Salad aux Fines Herbes

SERVES 6

The sight of a myriad of salads laid out on a picnic cloth in the country on a fine day is one of the great delights of midsummer. I like to bring as much variety as I can to the salady part of the meal, and this garlicky, herby pasta salad is wonderful. The tiny cubes of hard cheese make it slightly different – a feast.

Cook the pasta *al dente* and drain. Put under a tap of running water and toss so that all the starch is washed away. Shake dry. Mix with the peas and dress with the olive oil, adding more if necessary. Toss in the garlic, the herbs and the cheese, and mix well. Season to taste and keep in a cool place until ready to use.

350 g (12 oz) pasta quills or bows

175 g (6 oz) peas, cooked

4–5 tbls good-quality olive oil

1–2 cloves of garlic, crushed

3 tbls mixed herbs, chopped, such as chervil, chives, parsley, tarragon, dill and lovage

75 g (3 oz) hard cheese, cut into tiny cubes

salt and pepper

# Stuffed Courgettes

SERVES 6

I love giving picnic parties in the summer. The idea is to meet up with friends at an appointed spot, and everyone brings a picnic basket full of goodies. We lay everything out on a cloth and share. It is a brilliant idea because nobody has to do much work, and there's a minimum of clearing up to do.

Carefully scoop out the flesh inside the courgette halves so that they are boat-shaped. Put the sweetcorn and eggs into the food processor and blend to a rough purée. Add the herbs and the grated cheese and season to taste. Spoon into the courgette halves, put into an ovenproof dish and cover tightly with foil. Bake at gas mark 4/180°C/350°F until set, about 25–30 minutes. Remove from the dish and cool on a rack.

6 large courgettes, cut in half lengthwise

400 g (14 oz) can of sweetcorn, drained

2 eggs, beaten

2 tbls mixed herbs, chopped, such as chervil, chives, dill, mint and tarragon

50 g (2 oz) Gruyère cheese, finely grated

salt and pepper

# Midsummer Delights

*Dew was already on the paths. In the old oak-wood a mist was rising, and he hesitated, wondering whether one whiteness were a strand of fog or only campion flowers pallid in a cloud.*

. . .

*It was very still. The tree was tall and straggling. It had thrown its briers over a hawthorn bush, and its long streamers trailed thick, right down to the grass, splashing the darkness everywhere with great split stars, pure white. In bosses of ivory and in large splashed stars the roses gleamed on the darkness of foliage and stems and grass. Paul and Miriam stood close together, silent, and watched. Point after point the steady roses shone out to them, seeming to kindle something in their souls. The dusk came like smoke around, and still did not put out the roses.*

D. H. Lawrence, *Sons and Lovers*

## Chilled Fennel Soup

SERVES 6

The resonances of midsummer are unique to the season. Old country folk believed that this was a time of magic, when witches, elves and fairies were at large, and they used herbs and wild plants in various ways to protect themselves from their spells and antics. Fennel is one of the major herbs of midsummer, and is woven into garlands to hang over the door on St John's Eve (24 June) to ward off evil. Magic apart, it is a superb culinary herb and a sensational vegetable: this elegant soup proves it!

Soften the fennel and shallots in the butter, stirring, for 6–8 minutes. Add the potatoes and stir so that they, too, begin to soften, about 5 minutes. Add the stock, bring to the boil and simmer for 15–20 minutes until very soft. Liquidize, season to taste and cool. Stir in the cream and chill thoroughly. Serve sprinkled with chopped fennel leaves and a borage flower in the centre of each bowl.

1 large head of fennel, finely sliced

2 shallots, finely sliced

50 g (2 oz) butter

175 g (6 oz) new potatoes, peeled and sliced

900 ml (1½ pts) stock (see p. 149)

300 ml (½ pt) single cream

salt

*Garnish*

fennel leaves, chopped

borage flowers

*To see the world in a grain of sand*
*And a heaven in a wild flower.*
*Hold infinity in the palm of your hand*
*And eternity in an hour.*

William Blake

# Seafood Gratin

SERVES 6–8

This mixture of delectable fishes is delicately flavoured with fresh fennel leaves in a light creamy sauce, sprinkled with cheese and baked so that the topping is crisp. It is one of my favourite dishes for a special family occasion – simple yet memorable.

Lightly season the mackerel, cod or other fish, wrap in foil and bake at gas mark 5/190°C/375°F until firm, about 10–15 minutes. Cool, then remove all skin and bones from the fish and flake it. Prepare the shellfish as necessary, cooking the mussels (reserve the liquid) and shelling the prawns. Lightly steam the scallops and squid.

Make a stock from the skin, bones and prawn shells: cover them with water, adding the thyme, rosemary, tarragon and a little salt. Bring to the boil and simmer, covered, for 10 minutes. Leave to cool, then strain off.

Make the *sauce à la crème* with the fish stock and the strained mussel liquid, if any, instead of the milk, following the instructions on p. 148. Add a little garlic if you like, then stir in the chopped fennel.

Pour this sauce over the prepared fish and mix carefully together. Put into an ovenproof dish and sprinkle with the grated Parmesan cheese and dried breadcrumbs mixed together. Bake in a pre-heated oven at gas mark 6/200°C/400°F for 15 minutes.

750 g (1½ lb) selection of fish such as mackerel, cod fillet, halibut, swordfish

500 g (1 lb) selection of shellfish such as mussels, prawns, scallops, squid

1–2 sprigs of thyme

1–2 sprigs of rosemary

1–2 sprigs of tarragon

450 ml (¾ pt) *sauce à la crème* (see p. 148)

garlic to taste, crushed (optional)

3 tbls fennel leaves, chopped

50 g (2 oz) Parmesan cheese, grated

75 g (3 oz) dried breadcrumbs

# Tarragon and Tomato Soufflés

SERVES 4

Tarragon, to me, is a taste of high summer. It is one of the most distinctive of herbs, lending its unique fragrance to the fresh flavour of sun-ripened tomatoes. This dish looks as lovely as it tastes: each soufflé is cooked inside a half tomato shell. I like to serve it with baby new potatoes and a side salad of crisp lettuce.

Scoop the seeds and flesh out of the tomato halves and mix into the béchamel sauce. Add the tomato purée and blend until smooth in the blender. Mix in the tarragon and season lightly to taste. Fold in the stiffly beaten egg whites and pile into the tomato shells. Bake at gas mark 5/190°C/375°F until well risen and set, about 25 minutes. Serve immediately.

4 large beef tomatoes, cut in half

150 ml ($\frac{1}{4}$ pt) thick béchamel sauce (see p. 148)

1$\frac{1}{2}$ tbls tomato purée

1 tbls tarragon, chopped

salt and pepper

4 egg whites, stiffly beaten

# Garlicky Pasta with Summer Herbs

SERVES 4

This dish is really a celebration of summer's herbs. I have made this pasta dish often and it never contains the same mixture of herbs twice — I just pick what appeals to me on the day, whether it's chervil, tarragon, summer savory, mint, dill, coriander — or basil from my pots on the kitchen window-sill. Add these to pasta with garlic and pine nuts, and you have one of the most delicious and simple dishes imaginable.

Cook the pasta *al dente*. While it is cooking, stir the chopped herbs into the olive oil and add the crushed garlic. Drain the pasta, toss it with the herb oil and add the pine nuts. Season to taste, and toss again. Serve immediately on hot plates, with a bowl of grated Parmesan to hand around.

350 g (12 oz) pasta quills

1 tbls tansy, chopped

1 tbls lovage, chopped

1 tbls thyme, chopped

6 tbls olive oil

2 cloves of garlic, crushed

40 g (1$\frac{1}{2}$ oz) pine nuts

salt and pepper

Parmesan cheese, grated

# Mexican Shrimp Salad

SERVES 6

A light starter for a summery meal, this mixture of prawns and shrimps is spiced *à la Mexicano* – with hot chilli powder – so it is a prawn and avocado cocktail with a difference. Sour cream is added to the dressing to give it a cooling quality, and this is a lovely way to begin a meal alfresco on a summer's evening.

Combine all the shellfish and salad ingredients except the lettuce.

Mix the mayonnaise with the sour cream and stir in the chilli powder. Dress the salad with the mixture and place on a bed of lettuce in a shallow serving dish. Garnish with wedges of lemon.

500 g (1 lb) large prawns, shelled

250 g (8 oz) brown shrimps, peeled

250 g (8 oz) new potatoes, cooked and sliced

2 hard-boiled eggs, sliced

6 spring onions, finely sliced

flesh of 1 ripe avocado, diced

1 crisp lettuce, shredded

*Garnish*

lemon wedges

*For the dressing*

150 ml ($\frac{1}{4}$ pt) mayonnaise (see p. 148)

150 ml ($\frac{1}{4}$ pt) sour cream

$\frac{1}{4}$–$\frac{1}{2}$ tsp chilli powder

salt to taste

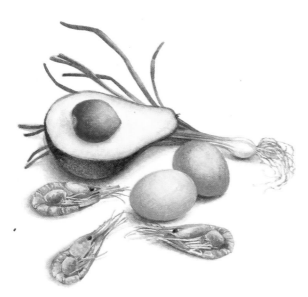

*I am the pure fragrance that comes from the earth and the brightness of fire I am. I am the life of all living beings, and the austere life of those who train their souls.*

Bhagavadgita

## Courgette Soufflé-omelette with Mixed Herbs

### SERVES 6

Always so impressive to look at, a soufflé-omelette is deceptively quick and easy to make, and is a special main course for a simple summer meal. Freshly picked courgettes are one of my very favourite summer vegetables, and make a delicious filling mixed with chopped herbs of your choice. This soufflé-omelette is exquisite served with baby new potatoes and runner beans, and a tossed green salad on the side.

Plunge the finely sliced courgettes into boiling water, simmer for 30 seconds, and drain thoroughly. Toss them in the butter with the herbs. Stir in the cream and heat through gently.

Beat the egg yolks and season with a little salt and pepper. Fold in the stiffly beaten whites, then the courgettes. Heat a little butter in a large, heavy-bottomed frying pan and pour the mixture in. Cook as for an omelette over a very gentle heat, so that the bottom does not burn, until the eggs begin to puff, about 5 minutes. Remove from the pan and bake in a pre-heated oven at gas mark 8/230°C/450°F for 2–3 minutes, so that it sets in the middle. Cut into 6 wedges and serve immediately on warmed plates.

250 g (8 oz) courgettes, finely sliced

a little unsalted butter

3 tbls mixed herbs, finely chopped

5 tbls single cream

salt and pepper

6 eggs, separated

a little butter

salt and pepper

# Rose Ice-cream

SERVES 4–6

An old-fashioned idea, perhaps, but why not use fragrant rose petals like they used to in the old days? They have a delicately perfumed taste that makes an irresistible ice-cream. Just for good measure, I garnish mine with wild rose petals: they not only make the dishes of ice-cream look exquisite, but are soft and luscious to eat as well.

Beat the cream until thick and fold in the icing sugar. Beat until it holds its shape and mix in the vanilla. Fold in the stiffly beaten egg whites. Put into a container and freeze for 1 hour.

Using a food processor, blend the rose petals with the sugar and wine until pulverized, about 1 minute. Fold into the soft ice-cream and re-freeze for several hours or overnight. Serve in tall glasses garnished with a slice of peach and a sprinkling of wild rose petals.

300 ml ($\frac{1}{2}$ pt) double cream

50 g (2 oz) icing sugar

2 tsp vanilla essence

2 egg whites, stiffly beaten

1 small bunch of rose petals (preferably red)

1 tbls caster sugar

1 small glass of rosé wine

*Garnish*

wild rose petals

peach slices

*If good we plant not, vice will fill the mind*
*And weeds despoil the space for flowers designed*
*The human heart ne'er knows a state of rest*
*Bad tends to worse and better tends to best*
*We either gain or lose, we sink and rise*
*Nor rests our struggling nature till it dies*

Nineteenth-century sampler

## Summery Buffets

I love at eventide to walk alone
Down narrow lanes o'erhung with dewy thorn
Where from the long grass underneath the snail
Jet black creeps out and sprouts his timid horn
I love to muse oer meadows newly mown
Where withering grass perfumes the sultry air
Where bees search round with sad and weary drone
In vain for flowers that bloomed but newly there
While in the juicey corn the hidden quail
Cries 'wet my foot' and hid as thoughts unborn
The fairy like and seldom-seen land rail
Utters 'craik craik' like voices underground
Right glad to meet the evenings dewy veil
And see the light fade into glooms around

John Clare, *Summer Moods*

# Marinated Crudités with Dips

SERVES 4

The buffet table is a great institution. It is one of the best ways of having a party because you have prepared all the food in advance, and can actually relax and enjoy the company of your friends. In the summer its added joy is that you can be outside: a large table set in the garden, laden with colourful and appetizing dishes, is a perfect centrepiece for enjoying a summer's day. These marinated crudités always cause enthusiastic comment, and are quite different from the ubiquitous raw chopped vegetable ... And as for the dips!

Prepare the vegetables: slice the fennel and the radishes; cut the carrots, courgettes and artichoke hearts into matchstick strips; cut the French beans into 2.5-cm (1-in) lengths and quarter the mushrooms.

Add 300 ml ($\frac{1}{2}$ pt) water to the marinade ingredients and boil for 10 minutes. Strain the hot marinade over the vegetables in a saucepan and leave until cold. Strain off the vegetables and arrange on a platter.

Take a yellow pepper, cut it across in thin slices and remove the seeds. Peel 6 small tomatoes and place them stem-side down. Cut almost all the way through with 4 crossing cuts to make 8 petals in each. Prise open. Decorate the vegetable platter with the yellow pepper rings and the tomato lilies. Serve with the following dips.

750 g (1$\frac{1}{2}$ lb) selection of fennel, white radishes, carrots, courgettes, artichoke hearts, French beans, button mushrooms, baby broad beans

*Garnish*

yellow pepper rings

tomato lilies (see below)

*For the marinade*

300 ml ($\frac{1}{2}$ pt) dry white wine

1 bay leaf

1 large sprig of thyme

150 ml ($\frac{1}{4}$ pt) olive oil

grated rind and juice of 1 lemon

3 tbls white wine vinegar

6 coriander seeds

2 chillies

6 black peppercorns, crushed

2.5-cm (1-in) piece of root ginger, grated

1 tbls salt

2 large cloves of garlic, crushed

1 tbls sugar

### Green Herb Dip

Put the mayonnaise into the food processor with the spring onions. Strip the leaves off the stems of the herbs and add them to the mayonnaise. Liquidize to a purée. Season to taste with lemon juice.

150 ml (¼ pt) mayonnaise (see p. 148)

2 spring onions, finely chopped

1 medium bunch of basil

1 medium bunch of dill

lemon juice to taste

### Garlicky Aubergine Dip

Bake the aubergine, whole, at gas mark 4/ 180°C/350°F until completely soft through, about 45–50 minutes. Cool, then skin, remove the flesh and purée in the food processor with the oil and garlic. Season to taste with salt and pepper, and stir in the chopped parsley. Chill. Thin out with more olive oil if necessary, to make it a dipping consistency. Sprinkle with paprika and garnish with lemon wedges.

1 large aubergine

5 tbls olive oil

2 large cloves of garlic, crushed

salt and pepper

2 tbls parsley, chopped

paprika

*Garnish*

lemon wedges

# Oeufs Mollets with Mint Mayonnaise

SERVES 4

This is a knock-out. I rave about soft-boiled eggs – cooked to perfection so that the whites are just set (*not* like leather) and the yolks runny. Mint is the freshest of all our summer herbs, and counteracts the richness of the eggs in their mayonnaise. Gorgeous with fresh bread and a crisp, leafy salad.

Put the eggs into a saucepan of cold water and bring to the boil. Simmer gently for 3 minutes, then plunge into cold water. Leave to cool completely, then shell carefully and cut in half. The yolks should be runny, the whites firm. Place cut-side up on a bed of shredded lettuce in a serving dish. Stir the chopped mint into the mayonnaise and spoon it over the eggs in the dish. Garnish with sprigs of mint and surround with baby tomatoes cut in half in a zigzag pattern.

6 eggs

3 sprigs of mint, finely chopped

300 ml ($\frac{1}{2}$ pt) mayonnaise (see p. 148)

*Garnish*

lettuce

sprigs of mint

baby tomatoes

# Baby Sweetcorn with Coriander

SERVES 4

Of all the dishes in this section, this is the one that has caused more comment and more demand for the recipe than any other. It is truly wonderful: oriental flavours of coriander and ginger, added to the sensational texture of baby sweetcorn poached in a yogurt sauce. I put the finishing touches of coriander leaves and carrot matchsticks in a decorative pattern over the top – and it looks as fabulous as it tastes.

In a large frying pan, heat the oil and gently sauté the baby sweetcorn in it for 7–8 minutes, stirring all the time so that they are well coated and beginning to soften. Remove from the pan. Add the onion to the oil in the pan and sauté it gently until soft, about 5 minutes. Stir in the coriander, garlic and ginger, and stir-fry together for a further 2 minutes. Then stir in two thirds of the yogurt and mix well. Return the baby sweetcorn to the pan and poach them gently in the sauce, covered but stirring from time to time, for a further 10 minutes. Remove the corn from the pan with a slotted spoon and cool.

Liquidize the cooled sauce to a smooth, thin consistency, and add to the remaining yogurt gradually, so that the sauce holds together. Spoon over the cooled sweetcorn and garnish with sprigs of coriander and carrot matchsticks when ready to serve.

4 tbls vegetable oil

500 g (1 lb) baby sweetcorn

1 onion, finely chopped

1 small bunch of coriander, chopped

2 cloves of garlic, crushed

2.5-cm (1-in) piece of root ginger, grated

150 ml ($\frac{1}{4}$ pt) natural yogurt

*Garnish*

sprigs of coriander

carrot matchsticks

# Sorrel and Tomato Roulade

SERVES 6

A party piece: a dish with fresh, refreshing tastes that looks far more difficult to achieve than it actually is. I use sorrel as much as I can while it is in season – it makes such delicious soups and sauces.

Grease a 33 × 24-cm (13½ × 9½-in) Swiss roll tin and line it with oiled greaseproof paper.

Heat the béchamel sauce gently and stir in the cheese. Cook very gently for 5 minutes, then season to taste with salt and pepper. Cook the sorrel in its own water until soft and well cooked down, about 5 minutes. Drain it thoroughly. Chop it, press it through a sieve to remove the stringy parts, and stir it into the sauce. Remove from the heat and stir in the egg yolks one by one. Beat the whites until they are very stiff, and fold into the mixture. Pour into the prepared tin and spread it evenly. Bake at gas mark 4/180°C/350°F for 18–20 minutes until firm.

As soon as you remove it from the oven, cover the roulade with a cloth and turn it upside down on to a wire tray. Peel away the paper and leave to cool.

Cook the peeled, chopped tomatoes in the oil for 3–4 minutes, then stir in the chopped herbs and cook for a further 5 minutes. Season to taste, remove from the pan and put into a sieve to cool and to drain off the juices. Mix with the tomato purée and leave until cold.

Spread this purée on to the roulade to within 1 cm (½ in) of the edges, and roll it up, using the cloth to help. Place on a serving dish and cover with cling-film. Chill thoroughly, and serve sliced, decorated with courgette roses.

300 ml (½ pt) béchamel sauce (see p. 148)

2 tbls Parmesan cheese, grated

salt and pepper

250 g (8 oz) sorrel, washed

4 eggs, separated

8 tomatoes, peeled and chopped

3 tbls olive oil

2 tbls mixed herbs, finely chopped

1 tbls tomato purée

*Garnish*

courgette roses

## Lemonade

MAKES 2 L (3½ PTS)

There is no drink that you can buy to touch fresh, home-made lemonade, and summer wouldn't be summer, as far as I'm concerned, if I didn't make several batches of the stuff for my family. Wonderfully lemony, it is the most refreshing drink in the world, especially when mixed with sparkling mineral water.

Pour 1.75 l (3 pts) boiling water over the lemons in a large basin. Add the sugar and stir in the tartaric and citric acids, and the salt. Stir until dissolved. Leave to stand for 36 hours, stirring from time to time. Strain off and bottle in clean containers. To serve, dilute with chilled sparkling mineral water.

6 lemons, sliced and chopped

1.5 kg (3 lb) sugar

25 g (1 oz) tartaric acid

25 g (1 oz) citric acid

½ tsp salt

*Then the broad bosom of the oceans keeps*
*An equal motion; swelling as it sleeps,*
*Then slowly sinking; curling to the strand,*
*Faint, lazy waves o'ercreep the rigid sand,*
*Or tap the tarry boat with gentle blow,*
*And back in silence, smooth and slow.*

George Crabbe, *Summer Sea*

# Ange aux Framboises

SERVES 8

No summer buffet party would be complete without at least one special dessert. For the most part I like to offer fresh soft fruits in season, just with sugar and cream, or else a fruit salad. But it's hard to resist both making and eating this gâteau. It is lightness itself, utterly mouth-watering, and a fitting finale to a summer buffet.

Add half of the cream of tartar to the sifted flour and sift it again. Add the rest of the cream of tartar and a pinch of salt to the beaten egg whites. Beat in the sifted sugar 2 tbls at a time, whisking as you do so, and then add the lemon juice and vanilla essence. Fold in the flour 2 tbls at a time and mix in well. Spoon the mixture into a well-greased cake tin, preferably one with a removable base. Bake at gas mark 5/190°C/375°F for 20 minutes, then turn the heat down to gas mark 3/170°C/325°F and bake for a further 20 minutes. Cool on a rack for 10 minutes, then turn out and cool completely.

Mix the raspberries with the caster sugar and leave for 10 minutes to draw out the juices. Slice the cooled cake into three tiers and arrange one third of the raspberries on the bottom layer. Cover with some of the whipped cream, and put the second layer on top. Repeat, reserving some cream for decoration, and pile the last of the raspberries over the top and around the edge of the gâteau. Chill for several hours. Just before serving, dust with icing sugar and decorate with the rest of the whipped cream, piping it into patterns.

2 tsp cream of tartar

75 g (3 oz) plain flour, sifted

pinch of salt

6 egg whites, stiffly beaten

175 g (6 oz) caster sugar, sifted

1 tbls lemon juice

1 tsp vanilla essence

750 g (1½ lb) raspberries

50 g (2 oz) caster sugar

300 ml (½ pt) double cream, whipped

icing sugar

# Raw Food

I often pulled my hat over my eyes to watch the rising of the lark or to see the hawk hang in the summer sky and the kite take its circles round the wood     I often lingered a minute on the woodland stile to hear the woodpigeons clapping their wings among the dark oaks     I hunted curious flowers in rapture and muttered thoughts in their praise     I loved the pasture with its rushes and thistles and sheep tracks     I adored the wild marshy fen with its solitary hernshaw sweeping along its melancholy sky     I wandered the heath in raptures among the rabbit burrows and golden blossomed furze     I dropt down on the thymy molehill or mossy eminence to survey the summer landscape

John Clare, *Prose*

# Avocado, Melon and Basil Cocktail

**SERVES 4**

Fruity and summery, this luscious cocktail makes a scrumptious starter, or even just a simple light lunch served with fresh granary bread and a crisp side salad. The unusual dressing, a purée of tomato, yogurt, garlic and mayonnaise, blends perfectly with the basil that permeates this dish. I eat a lot of raw food in the summer – all the salads and herbs and fruits are at their best, and, of course, this kind of 'cooking' has the advantage that it is easy, quick and, above all, cool to prepare!

Purée the tomatoes with the yogurt and stir in the mayonnaise and garlic. Season to taste with salt and pepper, and allow the dressing to stand for 30 minutes before using.

Combine the avocado, melon, raisins and basil, and toss with the dressing. Serve in tall glasses.

2 canned tomatoes

150 ml ($\frac{1}{4}$ pt) natural yogurt

2 tbls mayonnaise (see p. 148)

1 clove of garlic, crushed

salt and pepper

flesh of 1 large avocado, diced

half of a honeydew melon, balled or cut into cubes

75 g (3 oz) raisins

2 tbls basil leaves, shredded

## Tomato Pesto Slices

SERVES 4

Every summer I grow basil in pots on my kitchen window-sill, and I look after it with tender loving care. It is such a fabulous herb, and I grow enough each year to make my own pesto: that incredible, if unlikely, mixture of basil leaves, garlic, Parmesan cheese, olive oil and pine nuts. One of my favourite snacks is slices of sun-ripened tomatoes spread with pesto and placed on fresh bread. Try resisting it!

Slice the tomatoes. Cut the bread into squares the same size as the sliced tomatoes, and brush each one with olive oil. Place a slice of tomato on top of each square of bread and top each one with a little pesto. Arrange in a dish or on a platter, and garnish with sprigs of basil.

*To make the pesto:* Put the basil into the blender with the garlic, pine nuts and olive oil. Blend until smooth. Stir in the Parmesan cheese. Thin out with more oil if necessary.

250 g (8 oz) medium tomatoes, peeled

4 slices of bread, crusts removed

olive oil

*Garnish*

sprigs of basil

*For the pesto (makes 175 ml/6 fl oz)*

1 medium bunch of basil

2 large cloves of garlic, crushed

25 g (1 oz) pine nuts

4–6 tbls olive oil

25 g (1 oz) Parmesan cheese, grated

*And this is certain, if so be*
*You could just now my garden see,*
*The aspic of my flowers so bright*
*Would make you shudder with delight.*

*And if you voz to see my roziz*
*As is a boon to all men's noziz, –*
*You'd fall upon your back & scream –*
*'O Lawk! o criky! it's a dream!'*

Edward Lear, *For Lovers of Flowers and Gardens*

# Sweet and Sour Courgettes

SERVES 4

When courgettes are really fresh, I think they are sensational raw. They are delicate, crunchy and more-ish. Coated with a sweet and sour sauce, they make a delicious salad, especially served alongside the mushroom salad below. Or just have them with fresh, warm bread and a green salad – a beautiful, light lunch.

Liquidize the sugar, vinegar, soy sauce and tomato purée. Stir in 100 ml (4 fl oz) of water and simmer for 5 minutes. Add more soy if necessary. Cool.

Slice the courgettes paper-thin and put into a bowl. Toss with the sweet and sour sauce, and marinate for several hours. Serve garnished with sprigs of parsley.

2 tbls soft brown sugar

2 tbls vinegar

1 tbls soy sauce

1 tbls tomato purée

750 g (1½ lb) baby courgettes (include some yellow ones if available)

*Garnish*

sprigs of parsley

# Best Mushroom Salad

SERVES 4

This is truly my favourite mushroom salad. Raw mushrooms are whizzed in the food processor so that they look minced, and are then dressed in a curry mayonnaise. It sounds too simple to be so good, but it is epicurean.

Put the mushrooms into the food processor and whizz for a few seconds, until they look minced. Mix the mayonnaise with the curry paste and dress the mushrooms with the mixture. Put into a serving dish and garnish with a sprinkling of walnuts and sprigs of parsley.

350 g (12 oz) button mushrooms

4 tbls mayonnaise (see p. 148)

1–2 tsp curry paste

*Garnish*

40 g (1½ oz) walnuts, coarsely ground

sprigs of parsley

# Indonesian Vegetable Salad

SERVES 4

The slightly spicy, thick dressing for this salad has a peanut base to it, which gives it its Indonesian quality. Deliciously spiced with chilli, garlic and soy sauce, and with a hint of sweetness, it makes a really original and irresistible salad.

Grind the peanuts in a coffee grinder. Put into a bowl and add the chilli powder, garlic, soy sauce and lemon juice. Mix well. Gradually stir in the oil, 1 tbls at a time, until the sauce becomes smooth and thick. Add the sugar and leave to stand for a while before dressing the vegetables.

1 kg (2 lb) selection of beansprouts, French beans, cucumber, radishes, mange-tout, baby carrots, all cut into quite small pieces

50 g (2 oz) dry-roasted peanuts

$\frac{1}{2}$ tsp chilli powder

3 cloves of garlic, crushed

2 tbls soy sauce

1 tbls lemon juice

150 ml ($\frac{1}{4}$ pt) sesame oil

2 tsps dark-brown sugar

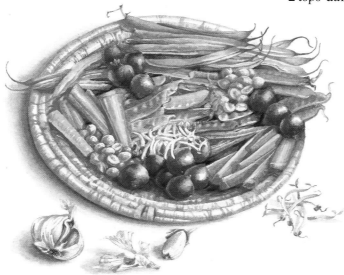

*If a traveller does not meet with one who is his better, or his equal, let him firmly keep to his solitary journey; there is no companionship with a fool.*

Buddha

# Red and Green Salad

SERVES 4

Grated vegetables make fabulous salads. This combination of grated courgette and carrot is not only pretty to look at, but has a mouth-watering texture and wonderful flavour. A hint of garlic in the mayonnaise brings out the best in the two vegetables.

Using a food processor, grate the carrots and the courgettes coarsely and mix well together. Stir the crushed garlic into the mayonnaise and mix well. Dress the raw vegetables with the garlic mayonnaise, and leave to stand for a good 30 minutes before serving, so that the flavour of the garlic can fully permeate the salad.

250 g (8 oz) baby carrots

250 g (8 oz) courgettes

1 large clove of garlic, crushed

150 ml ($\frac{1}{4}$ pt) mayonnaise (see p. 148)

# Baby Vegetable Kebabs

SERVES 4

People love these little kebabs of raw vegetables. They look pretty and colourful served with flavoured mayonnaises and dipping sauces of your choice. They are an excellent party-piece, lovely to eat alfresco with a bottle of chilled white wine to accompany them.

Cut the vegetables and fruit into bite-sized cubes and spear on to kebab sticks. Shred the lettuce and dress it with the vinaigrette. Place in the bottom of a large, shallow dish and place the kebabs decoratively on top.

Mix half of the mayonnaise with the grated cheese and onion. Mix the other half with the mint. Put into two separate bowls and serve as dips alongside the kebabs. You can also serve them with the dipping sauces on p. 28.

1 kg (2 lb) selection of button mushrooms, stoned olives, skinned baby tomatoes, courgettes, cucumber, pineapple

1 large crisp lettuce

5 tbls vinaigrette

300 ml ($\frac{1}{2}$ pt) mayonnaise (see p. 148)

25 g (1 oz) Parmesan cheese, finely grated

1 tsp onion, grated

1 tbls mint leaves, chopped

# Summer

## Seasonal Side Vegetables

Full summer comes; June brings the longest day.
All country dwellers know the small despair
Of the year's summit; but the yeoman now
Has little time for vain regrets to spare.
There's work enough for him and all his folks;
He watches for the flowering of his hay;
Knows that cleared land is ready for the plough;
Washes his empty sheds with cleansing lime
While herds at pasture fatten to their prime,
With fisking tails in shade beneath the oaks.

V. Sackville-West, *The Land*

40

## Sorrel with Peas

SERVES 4

Sorrel grows abundantly in my herb garden and I pick it furiously throughout the summer. Luckily it freezes well, so it's lovely to have it later on in the year as a reminder of sunnier days. Sorrel combines deliciously with peas – a sharp taste with a sweet one. This is a fabulous side vegetable.

Wash the sorrel and cook it in its own water, which will take only 1–2 minutes. Drain thoroughly, chop and mix with the béchamel sauce so that it is like a purée. Season to taste with salt, pepper and nutmeg and mix with the hot, cooked peas.

1 large bunch of sorrel

5 tbls béchamel sauce (see p. 148)

salt and pepper

ground nutmeg

250 g (8 oz) peas, cooked

## Deep fried Green Beans

SERVES 4

The simple device of deep-frying runner beans transforms their flavour. It's difficult to describe exactly, but it's a wonderful taste and well worth trying. Add a touch of the orient with soy, ginger and garlic.

Trim the beans and slice them. Drop into very hot oil, a handful at a time, and deep-fry until slightly wrinkled, about 3–4 minutes. Drain on kitchen paper and keep them hot. Mix the garlic and ginger into the soy sauce, and just before serving toss with the beans.

For a simpler dish, just sprinkle the cooked beans with a little sea salt. French beans are also delicious cooked in this way.

350 g (12 oz) runner beans

vegetable oil for deep-frying

1 clove of garlic, very finely chopped

a little grated root ginger

1–2 tbls soy sauce

# Broad Beans with Caraway

SERVES 4

Baby broad beans are one of the great delights of midsummer. Tender and succulent, full of flavour – I love them. Just to ring the changes, try tossing them in butter with a few caraway seeds – it's memorable.

Cook the beans in salted, boiling water until tender. Drain. Toss with the butter until well coated. Sprinkle in the caraway seeds, toss again, and serve.

500 g (1 lb) baby broad beans, shelled

25 g (1 oz) unsalted butter

2 tsps caraway seeds

# New Potatoes Baked in Butter with Herbs

SERVES 4

Baking little new potatoes in foil with herbs and butter seals in their flavour and makes them quite tantalizing. They are delicious with fish dishes, and make a plain omelette and salad into a meal.

Put the potatoes into an ovenproof dish with a tight-fitting lid and toss with the herbs. Sprinkle a little sea salt over the top and dot with the butter. Cover the dish with foil and put on the lid so that it is well sealed. Bake at gas mark 6/200°C/400°F until the potatoes are tender but still crisp, about 45–50 minutes.

750 g (1½ lb) small new potatoes, scrubbed

2 tbls mixed herbs, finely chopped

sea salt

40 g (1½ oz) butter

# Baby Courgettes Beurre Noisette

SERVES 4

Here are two of my favourite things brought together in one fabulous dish: tender baby courgettes and *beurre noisette*, nut-brown butter. These courgettes go with almost anything, although I can eat them as a meal in themselves, with a side salad and fresh bread to mop up the juices.

Steam the courgettes for a few minutes until tender but still crisp. Meanwhile, melt the butter and continue to heat it, stirring, until it turns nut brown. Add the vinegar to the pan and let it froth and rage around a bit, and then pour over the hot courgettes. Toss thoroughly and serve.

625 g (1¼ lb) baby courgettes, very thinly sliced

75 g (3 oz) butter

1 tbls wine vinegar

*It is not good for all your wishes to be fulfilled; through sickness you recognize the value of health, through evil the value of good, through hunger satisfaction, through exertion the value of rest.*

*If man is moderate and contented, then even age is no burden; if he is not, then even youth is full of cares.*

Plato

43

# Light Fruit Desserts

The south-west wind how pleasant in the face
It breathes while sauntering in a musing pace
I roam these new-ploughed fields and by the side
Of this old wood where happy birds abide
And the rich blackbird through his golden bill
Litters wild music when the rest are still
Now luscious comes the scent of blossomed beans
That oer the path in rich disorder leans
Mid which the bees in busy songs and toils
Load home luxuriantly their yellow spoils
The herd cows toss the molehills in their play
And often stand the strangers steps at bay
Mid clover blossoms red and tawney white
Strong scented with the summers warm delight

John Clare, *Beans in Blossom*

44

# Blackcurrant Shortcake

SERVES 4

Every year, when they come into season, I swear that blackcurrants are my favourite fruit, although how one can possibly choose between blackcurrants, mangoes, wild strawberries... But certainly blackcurrants rank high on any list of gastronomic fruits: they make a marvellous jam, a beautiful crumble, and this shortcake, which is irresistible.

Sprinkle the prepared blackcurrants with the caster sugar and toss until well coated. Put into the bottom of an ovenproof dish. Sift the flour with the baking powder. Cream the butter and rub in the sugar until smooth and creamy. Mix in the flour mixture with your fingertips until it is crumbly. Spread this mixture over the top of the blackcurrants and press it down lightly. Mark a criss-cross pattern over the top with a fork. Bake at gas mark 4/180°C/350°F for 20–25 minutes, and cool. Serve cold, with cream.

350 g (12 oz) blackcurrants, topped and tailed

2 tbls caster sugar

125 g (4 oz) plain flour

$\frac{1}{2}$ tsp baking powder

40 g (1$\frac{1}{2}$ oz) butter

65 g (2$\frac{1}{2}$ oz) soft brown sugar

# Melon and Ginger Ice-cream

SERVES 4–6

Once tasted, never forgotten. This exquisite dessert is more like a sorbet than an ice-cream, with its texture of melon and the lightness of yogurt that make it so summery. The surprise is the ginger: it highlights the delicacy of the melon, and lingers on the tastebuds. Make a good supply of it – it's very popular!

Add the chopped melon to the slivered ginger and mix into the yogurt. Beat the egg yolks and fold them in. Beat the whites until stiff, then fold in the caster sugar and beat again until very stiff. Fold into the fruit and yogurt mixture and freeze.

1 cantaloup or Ogen melon, de-seeded and finely chopped

125 g (4 oz) stem ginger, slivered

300 ml ($\frac{1}{2}$ pt) thick-set natural yogurt

2 eggs, separated

50 g (2 oz) caster sugar

45

# Bilberry Tart

SERVES 6–8

If you live in the north of the country, you may be lucky enough to find bilberries growing in the wild; southerners have to make do with picking them off the supermarket shelf. This recipe, based on a classic French method for a dessert fruit tart, takes time to prepare, but it is worth every minute. It is a dessert you will never forget.

Put the sugar and 300 ml (½ pt) water into a heavy saucepan and boil until it is syrupy, about 5 minutes. Add the prepared bilberries to the pan and poach them gently for 5 minutes. Drain, reserving the syrup, and allow them to cool. Add 5 tbls of the syrup to the redcurrant jelly and boil hard for 3 minutes, stirring, until thick. Cool a little, then brush the base of the pre-cooked pie shell with this glaze. Allow to cool.

Spread 450 ml (¾ pt) of the *crème patissière* over the base of the prepared pie shell so that it is about 1 cm (½ in) thick. Place the bilberries over the top evenly, and finally brush with the rest of the glaze, reheating it if necessary. Allow to cool completely, and serve chilled.

*To make the* crème patissière: Beat the sugar into the egg yolks gradually and whisk until pale yellow and thick, about 2–3 minutes. Mix in the flour. Gradually pour on the boiling milk, stirring all the time. Transfer the mixture into a heavy-bottomed pan and heat gently until it thickens, stirring all the time. Let it bubble very gently for 2–3 minutes to cook the flour. Finally, stir in the butter and vanilla, and leave to cool.

75 g (3 oz) sugar

500 g (1 lb) bilberries, stoned

5 tbls each of redcurrant jelly and syrup from the cooked fruit

25-cm (10-in) sweet crust pie shell (see p. 149), baked blind

*For the* crème patissière *(makes 600 ml/1 pt)*

175 g (6 oz) caster sugar

5 egg yolks

75 g (3 oz) plain flour, sifted

450 ml (¾ pt) milk, boiling

15 g (½ oz) butter

2–3 tsp vanilla essence

# Perfect Pavlova

SERVES 6

The legendary ballerina Anna Pavlova was offered this sublime dessert when she visited Australia in the thirties, and it has gone down in the annals of classic desserts bearing her name. It makes a wonderful finale to a summer party or a special meal – light meringue sandwiched with fresh fruits of the season and a little whipped cream. Only one drawback: it vanishes. So make two for good measure!

Gradually beat the caster sugar into the stiffly beaten egg whites and beat again until very stiff. Add the cornflour, vinegar and vanilla, and beat again. Pipe or spoon on to greased greaseproof paper or rice paper on a baking tray. Make a second meringue in the same way. Bake them in a pre-heated oven at gas mark 2/150°C/300°F for 1–1¼ hours. Lift the meringues carefully on to a rack to cool.

Arrange the fruit on top of one layer of the meringue (reserve some for the top), and cover with whipped cream. Place the second meringue layer on top and dust with icing sugar. Finally, decorate with more whipped cream and some of the reserved fruit.

175 g (6 oz) caster sugar

3 egg whites, stiffly beaten

1 tsp cornflour

1 tsp vinegar

1 tsp vanilla essence

750 g (1½ lb) selection of peaches, strawberries, nectarines, raspberries, whitecurrants, peeled and stoned, topped and tailed, etc.

300 ml (½ pt) double cream, whipped

1 tbls icing sugar, sifted

*All who joy would win must share – happiness is born a twin.*

Byron

# Wild Strawberry Syllabub

SERVES 4

The syllabub is as English as apple pie, a traditional, pastoral recipe that dates back to the seventeenth century. To my mind, it is the best way ever invented for eating cream – the sharp edge of lemon juice cuts across its richness, and makes a mouth-watering background to the delicate taste of wild strawberries. If you don't have access to *fraises des bois* (I cultivate a small patch in my garden for this purpose alone), ordinary strawberries make a delicious syllabub, too.

Mix the white wine, kirsch, lemon rind and juice, and leave them to stand for several hours or overnight. Strain. Add the sugar, and stir until it dissolves. Pour in the cream slowly, stirring all the time, and add a little nutmeg. Whisk until it thickens, being careful not to overdo it and curdle the mixture.

Hull the strawberries. Cut the wild ones into half if they are big ones, leaving the little ones whole. Toss with the icing sugar, and fold into the cream, leaving a few aside for decoration. Blend the ordinary strawberries to a purée in the blender, and spoon one quarter of this purée into the bottom of 4 tall glasses. Carefully pour the prepared syllabub over the top, and serve chilled, decorated with the remaining strawberries.

1 small glass of white wine

2 tbls kirsch

pared rind of $\frac{1}{2}$ lemon

juice of 1 lemon

50 g (2 oz) caster sugar

300 ml ($\frac{1}{2}$ pt) double cream

ground or grated nutmeg

125 g (4 oz) wild strawberries

175 g (6 oz) ordinary strawberries

icing sugar

## Late Summer Pudding

SERVES 4

Summer pudding is one of our great national dishes – it does much to redeem English cookery, in my opinion. So simple to make, so delicious to eat. I have tried varying the fruits as summer goes by, using wild strawberries and raspberries that ripen in August, and then the first blackberries along with autumn strawberries. It's *carte blanche*, really: the basic idea is so good that you can experiment endlessly with the fruits. You may want to serve it with *crème Chantilly*, rather than the usual pouring cream.

Mix the prepared fruits with the sugar and put into a saucepan. Add 150 ml ($\frac{1}{4}$ pt) water and simmer for 6–8 minutes. Cool. Meanwhile, line a dish around the sides with rectangles of bread, up to the full height of the dish, and fill in the bottom with triangles of bread so that they make a perfect fit. Lift the fruit out of the juice with a slotted spoon and fill the mould with it. Add a little more juice at the end, but not too much, otherwise the pudding becomes runny and the bread too soft to hold its shape when turned out. Cover the top with more triangles of bread. Place a plate on top of it and then a 500-g (1-lb) weight. Put the pudding in the fridge for several hours or overnight. Then invert it, and turn it out on to a plate.

*To make the* crème Chantilly: Whip the cream until it begins to thicken. Add the icing sugar. Continue beating until it holds its shape lightly, and stir in the vanilla. Mix well, and keep chilled until ready to serve.

875 g ($1\frac{3}{4}$ lb) fruit such as wild strawberries, wild raspberries, whitecurrants, redcurrants, bilberries, dewberries, early blackberries, late strawberries, cherries, all topped and tailed, pitted, etc.

150 g (5 oz) sugar

thin slices white bread, crusts cut off

*For the* crème Chantilly

150 ml ($\frac{1}{4}$ pt) double cream

2 tbls icing sugar

1 tsp vanilla essence

49

# Autumn

# Autumn

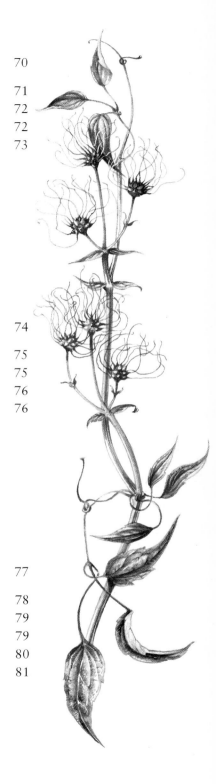

## Harvest Festival

*It rains, and nothing stirs within the fence*
*Anywhere through the orchard's untrodden, dense*
*Forest of parsley. The great diamonds*
*Of rain on the grass blades there is none to break,*
*Or the fallen petals further down to shake...*

Edward Thomas, *It Rains*

54

# Chanterelles with Black-eyed Beans

SERVES 4

Chanterelles usually grow near or in beech woods, so keep your eyes skinned for these honey-coloured, cone-shaped fungi. They are the kings of wild mushrooms: highly prized by French chefs but all too often ignored by the English. Their nutty flavour is exquisite – ordinary mushrooms pale into insignificance by comparison. Cooked in butter and tossed into black-eyed beans with oriental spices, they are delectable.

First prepare the soaked beans. Drain them, place in a large saucepan with ample water to cover, and bring to the boil. Simmer gently for about 20 minutes, until soft and tender but not mushy. Drain and cool a little, then mix in the ginger, garlic and sauces. Keep warm.

Slice the chanterelles and cook them in the butter over a medium heat until cooked through but still slightly crisp in texture, about 5–6 minutes. Toss with the black-eyed beans, check the seasoning, and serve warm or cold.

250 g (8 oz) black-eyed beans, soaked overnight

1-cm ($\frac{1}{2}$-in) piece of root ginger, finely grated

2 cloves of garlic, crushed

2 tbls hoisin sauce

1 tbls soy sauce

500 g (1 lb) chanterelles, washed and trimmed

125 g (4 oz) butter

## Gravlaks Table

SERVES 8

This table is the grand finale of the salmon season. It is my perennial late summer special, a spread of lusciously marinated fish with a gorgeous sauce and side dishes of vegetable and pasta salads. The simple marinade of sugar, salt and dill is a traditional Scandinavian recipe, and, to my mind, creates a delicacy even better than smoked salmon. A classic.

Prepare the fish: leaving the skin on, divide the fish into two equal parts. Mix the sugar together with the salt and freshly ground black pepper, and sprinkle over the surface of half of the salmon, laid in a dish skin-side down. Chop two thirds of the dill coarsely and scatter over the top. Place the other fillet over it, skin-side up, and cover the dish with foil. Put a weight on the top and place in the bottom of the fridge on a mid-thermostat setting. Leave for 3–4 days, basting daily with the juices that ooze out.

To serve, wipe the fish clean and remove the skin. Cut with a sharp knife into very thin slivers. Arrange on a serving dish and sprinkle with the rest of the dill, finely chopped, and a little more freshly ground black pepper. Serve with gravlaks sauce.

*To make the gravlaks sauce:* Mix the mustard, sugar, salt, pepper and vinegar in a bowl, and mix in the oil a little at a time to make a thick mayonnaise-type mixture. Stir in the dill.

750 g ($1\frac{1}{2}$ lb) salmon, filleted

5 tbls soft light-brown sugar

4 tbls salt

freshly ground black pepper

1 large bunch of dill

*For the gravlaks sauce*

4 tbls mild smooth mustard

2 tbls brown sugar

salt and freshly ground black pepper

2 tbls white wine vinegar

150 ml ($\frac{1}{4}$ pt) light vegetable oil

3–4 tbls dill, finely chopped

For the Gravlaks Table

little potatoes in sour cream, julienned cucumber and celeriac vinaigrette, calabrese florets with pasta twists in vinaigrette, little cubes of hard cheese, green salad, rye crispbread, king prawns to garnish the dishes

## Samphire with Dipping Sauces

SERVES 4

If you can obtain samphire, a highly
seasonal delicacy, pounce on it. This
asparagus of the seashore is epicurean,
with a taste and texture all its own, unforgettable with dipping sauces either hot or
cold. If you want to pick it yourself, go
prepared for the mud-flats – in old clothes
and Wellington boots, and armed with
plastic bags for the plunder. You'll probably need a bath when you get home, but
it'll be worth it!

Plunge the samphire into boiling water –
unsalted because the samphire tastes of
the sea – and cook for 10 minutes. Drain
and serve immediately on a hot platter, as
samphire loses its heat very quickly. Hold-
ing it by the root end, dip the green part
into melted butter or one of the dips on
p. 28 and pull the succulent covering off
the inner fibre with your teeth.

You can dip hot samphire into melted
butter just as you do asparagus and vary it
as you like: add a touch of garlic or some
finely chopped herbs (or both) to taste. Or
heat the butter until it is nut brown and
nutty in taste.

Samphire is also good cold, dipped into
mayonnaise with garlic and herbs added
in whatever combination you prefer.

1 kg (2 lb) samphire,
well washed

# Crispy Fried Puffball Steaks

SERVES 4

If you're out on an early morning walk and you come across a place where puffballs grow, take them home for this memorable autumn breakfast! The mushroom slices are coated with egg and breadcrumbs, then deep-fried until crisp. Served with grilled tomatoes and a poached egg, some granary toast and coffee, this gets the day off to a brilliant start.

Cut the puffball into slices about 5 mm ($\frac{1}{4}$ in) thick, so that they are more or less steak-size. Season the beaten eggs with salt and pepper. Heat the oil to chip heat, 220°C/425°F. Dip the puffball steaks into the beaten eggs and then into the breadcrumbs so that they are coated all over. Deep-fry them in the hot oil until golden and crisp, about half a minute. Drain and keep warm. Serve as soon as possible.

1 medium puffball

2 eggs, beaten

salt and pepper

vegetable oil for deep-frying

75 g (3 oz) wholemeal breadcrumbs

*Garnish*

sprigs of parsley

# Walnut Shortbread

SERVES 8

Sitting by the first log fire of the autumn, it's tea-time, and a plate of crumbly shortbread made with fresh walnuts from the garden stands by the teapot. Not for long, though — it is eagerly devoured by all the family and vanishes in no time at all.

Sift the flour with the baking powder and mix in the semolina. Stir in the chopped walnuts. Cream the butter with the sugar. Crumble with the flour mixture until thoroughly mixed. Press into a well-greased 20-cm (8-in) round cake tin and bake at gas mark 4/180°C/350°F until golden on top, about 25–30 minutes. Mark into 8 triangles and cool on a rack. Break into portions when completely cooled.

175 g (6 oz) plain flour

$\frac{1}{2}$ tsp baking powder

50 g (2 oz) semolina

50 g (2 oz) walnuts, chopped

150 g (5 oz) butter or margarine

65 g ($2\frac{1}{2}$ oz) caster sugar

# Crab-apple Cake

SERVES 8–10

I have a little harvest of bright-pink crab-apples every year – so pretty to look at and yet so sour! I like to make jelly with them – the best of all our wild jellies, I always think – and, until I tried this cake, that was all I used them for. Light and moist, fruity with a tang of cinnamon, it is delicious with a cup of tea or as the pudding course served with custard.

Sift the flour with the salt, bicarbonate and cinnamon. Rub in the butter or margarine until the mixture resembles breadcrumbs. Stir in the sugar.

Cut the crab-apples into quarters and remove the seeds. Chop the fruit and mix it into the cake base. Break in the eggs and stir thoroughly with a spoon. Do not beat. Bake in a pre-heated oven at gas mark 4/ 180°C/350°F until a knife comes out clean from the centre, about 45–50 minutes. Cool on a rack and dredge with icing sugar just before serving.

250 g (8 oz) self-raising flour

pinch of salt

pinch of bicarbonate of soda

1 tsp ground cinnamon

150 g (5 oz) butter or margarine

125 g (4 oz) light-brown sugar

500 g (1 lb) crab-apples

2 eggs

icing sugar

*Seek not to have that everything should happen as you wish, but wish for everything to happen as it actually does happen, and you will be serene.*

Epictetus

# The Larder Shelf

There was a day, ere yet the autumn closed,
When, ere her wintry ware, the earth reposed,
When from the yellow weed the feathery crown,
Light as the curling smoke fell slowly down;
When the winged insect settled in our sight,
And waited wind to recommence her flight;
When the white river was a silver sheet,
And on the ocean slept th'unanchored fleet.

George Crabbe, *Peter Grimes*

# Pickled Samphire

MAKES 2 L (4 PTS)

It's well worth making the most of the samphire crop. It grows abundantly on mud-flats near the sea, and you can gather it by the fistful – if you're prepared to get pretty muddy in the process! Samphire, pickled in spiced vinegar, makes a wonderful addition to a ploughman's lunch, and is really delicious with hard English cheeses.

Pick the young shoots of samphire that grow as a single stem, when they are about 15–20 cm (6–8 in) tall. Chop them into 2.5-cm (1-in) lengths. Put into clean screw-top jars and cover with spiced vinegar (below). Seal the jars thoroughly and store for 6–8 weeks before using.

*To make the spiced vinegar:* Put the vinegar and spices into a saucepan. Cover and heat gently. Leave on the lowest possible heat for 2 hours. Allow to cool in the pan, then strain off.

1 kg (2 lb) samphire, well washed

*For the spiced vinegar*

1 l (2 pts) malt vinegar

2 tbls whole cloves

2 tbls allspice berries

2 tbls white peppercorns

5-cm (2-in) piece of root ginger

2 × 7.5-cm (3-in) stick of cinnamon

# Blackberry Vinegar

MAKES 1.5 L (2½ PTS)

In years when blackberries are exceptionally plentiful, and I've made all the other goodies that are so much a feature of autumnal food, I make a supply of blackberry vinegar. It makes an exquisite salad dressing, with oil and a touch of soy sauce.

Select a wide-necked jar (Kilner jars are ideal for the purpose) and wash it thoroughly. Pick over the blackberries and put them into the bottom. Cover with the vinegar and seal the jar. Shake well and leave to stand for 2 weeks, shaking daily. Strain off the vinegar into a bottle and it is ready to use.

1 l (2 pts) white wine vinegar

250 g (8 oz) blackberries, washed

## Dried Mushrooms

This is probably the best way of preserving wild mushrooms. They retain their flavour beautifully, are easy to dry, and store away neatly. So make the most of the mushroom harvest – an expedition to the woods or fields with a large flat basket is an autumn experience not to be missed. I love it and so do my children.

If we lived in a civilized climate, we could dry our crop of wild mushrooms in the sun, but, alas, we must resort to our stoves and boilers. Clean and trim the mushrooms. Place them on newspaper and put in a warm place such as the airing cupboard or over the boiler. Spread them out so that they are not touching. Leave them for a few days and they will shrink, wrinkle and eventually become brittle. When they are completely dried out, pack them into paper or plastic bags.

Alternatively, thread the mushrooms on a fine string between circles of thin card, and hang them in a warm dry place such as the airing cupboard or over a radiator or night storage heater. When they are quite dry and brittle, store them in paper or plastic bags.

To reconstitute them, soak them in water for up to 24 hours, and use as for fresh mushrooms in soups, stuffings and casseroles, or in a stir-fry of mixed vegetables.

## Marrow, Pineapple and Ginger Jam

**MAKES 4.5 KG (9 LB)**

I have been making this recipe for years, and we never tire of it. It is an exotic jam with a translucent yellow colour and a silky texture. The usual autumnal glut of marrows comes into its own but in a different, original way. This jam is fabulous on fresh bread warm from the oven – a real tea-time treat.

Mix the marrow and pineapple together. Make alternating layers of fruit and sugar in a preserving pan. Leave overnight to extract the juice. Add the ginger if using.

Bring to the boil and boil rapidly, stirring occasionally, until setting point is reached, about 15–20 minutes. Leave to stand for 5 minutes before pouring into warm, clean jars. Cover and seal.

3 kg (6 lb) marrow, skinned, de-seeded and cubed

500 g (1 lb) pineapple, skinned, cored and cut into small chunks

250 g (8 oz) stem ginger, sliced (optional)

3 kg (6 lb) sugar

# Lemon and Ginger Shred

MAKES 5 KG (10 LB)

Once I'm in the swing of making autumn preserves for the larder shelf, my thoughts turn to marmalade. It's so satisfying to have a selection of interesting home-made ones, and this is one of our family favourites. Delicate in flavour, it is a pretty, pale translucent gold, just like evening light filtering through falling leaves.

Cut the lemons in half and squeeze the juice. Place the pips in a muslin bag. Slice the fruit finely and place in a preserving pan with the juice, the muslin bag and 3 l (5–6 pts) of water. Simmer gently until tender, about 1½–2 hours. Squeeze the muslin bag to extract the juice before removing it. Cool a little.

Add the sugar and stir until dissolved. Return to the heat, bring to the boil and boil rapidly to setting point. Add the ginger. Remove any scum and allow to cool until a thin skin forms on the top. Stir gently, then pour into warmed jars, cover and seal.

1.5 kg (3 lb) lemons

3 kg (6 lb) sugar

175 g (6 oz) stem ginger, finely sliced

# Favourite Food for Children

Coldly, sadly descends
The autumn-evening! The field
Strewn with its dank yellow drifts
Of withered leaves, and the elms,
Fade into dimness apace.
Silent; – hardly a shout
From a few boys late at their play!
The lights come out in the street,
In the school-room windows; – but cold,
Solemn, unlighted, austere,
Through the gathering darkness, arise
The chapel walls...

Matthew Arnold, *Rugby Chapel*

## Plate Pancake Pizzas

SERVES 4 (MAKES 2 PIZZAS)

The joy of this pizza is the simplicity of the base, which is like a thick pancake. You can, of course, vary the topping according to taste, but this version is particularly popular with my brood, especially as the days start to get colder and they appreciate warming, nourishing food like this.

Liquidize the flour with the egg yolks, milk and vegetable oil, and put to one side for 2 hours. Then beat the egg whites stiffly and fold into the batter. Put half of the mixture into a lightly greased, heavy frying pan and fry for 3–4 minutes on each side, until cooked through and golden. Make a second pancake in the same way.

Line two 20-cm (8-in) flan tins with the pancakes so that the edges curl up to form a surround for the pizza filling. Lay the sliced tomatoes on the pancake base and cover with a layer of mushrooms. Season with salt and pepper, and sprinkle with the dried thyme. Make a pattern over the top with the strips of mozzarella, and finally sprinkle with the Parmesan. Bake in a pre-heated oven for 15–20 minutes at gas mark 4/180°C/350°F. Cut each pizza in half and serve piping hot.

150 g (5 oz) plain flour

2 eggs, separated

150 ml (¼ pt) milk and water mixed

1 tbls vegetable oil

350 g (12 oz) tomatoes, skinned and sliced

175 g (6 oz) mushrooms, sliced

salt and pepper

1 tbls dried thyme

75 g (3 oz) mozzarella cheese, cut into strips

25 g (1 oz) Parmesan cheese, grated

# Crusty Cheese Pudding

SERVES 4

A perfect supper dish for hungry kids as the evenings draw in, and we light the first fire to keep off the chill. This is luscious, filling food which fends off feelings of gloom as the remnants of summer dissolve into the mists of autumn.

Cut the crusts off the bread and spread the slices with butter or margarine. Cut each slice into 8 strips. Put a layer in a greased baking dish and arrange the rest of the strips upright around the sides. Mix the beaten eggs with the rest of the ingredients and pour into the centre. Bake at gas mark 4/180°C/350°F for 30 minutes. Allow to stand for a few minutes before serving.

4 slices of bread

butter or margarine

2 eggs, beaten

300 ml ($\frac{1}{2}$ pt) milk or single cream

1 tsp salt

$\frac{1}{2}$ tsp mustard

freshly ground black pepper

250 g (8 oz) Cheddar cheese, grated

# Cauliflower Toad

SERVES 4

To make a change from toad in the hole, try this on your kids. The lightly steamed cauliflower florets in crisp, light Yorkshire pudding batter make a scrumptious autumn supper. Serve with coleslaw or a vegetable gratin, with the blackberry sorbet on p. 78 to follow.

Liquidize the flour, salt, egg and milk thoroughly and allow to stand for an hour.

Pour the vegetable oil into a 25-cm (10-in) square metal baking tin and heat through in a pre-heated oven at gas mark 7/220°C/425°F until it begins to smoke. Put the cauliflower florets in, cover with the batter, and cook for 10 minutes. Turn the heat down to gas mark 5/190°C/375°F and cook for a further 25–35 minutes, until puffed and golden.

125 g (4 oz) plain flour, sifted

$\frac{1}{4}$ tsp salt

1 egg

300 ml ($\frac{1}{2}$ pt) milk

3 tbls vegetable oil

1 cauliflower, cut into florets and steamed

# Brownies

MAKES 16

Tea time in autumn wouldn't be the same without brownies. Soft and chocolatey, these have the added surprise of chocolate drops, only half-melted, at the bottom. We have demolished countless brownies over the years, and they never lose their popularity in the slightest. This is my very best version of a classic American goodie.

Beat the eggs with the sugar until thick and smooth. Melt the chocolate with the margarine over hot water. Add this to the egg mixture and stir well. Beat in the flour and fold in the chocolate drops. Bake in a well-greased, 20-cm (8-in) square baking tin at gas mark 4/180°C/350°F until a knife comes out clean from the centre, about 20–25 minutes. Cool on a rack and cut into squares after about 10 minutes. Remove from the tin when cold.

2 eggs

175 g (6 oz) caster sugar

175 g (6 oz) plain chocolate

125 g (4 oz) margarine

65 g (2½ oz) plain flour, sifted

125 g (4 oz) plain chocolate drops

# Crispy Mushroom Morsels

My children are delighted with these tasty little mushrooms wrapped in rice paper and deep-fried until they are crisp and golden. The mushrooms retain all of their flavour cooked in this way, and in my family this is a favourite high tea snack.

Wrap the required number of mushrooms in little squares of rice paper, and ensure that each parcel is securely sealed by moistening the free edges down. Fry in very hot oil (220°C/425°F) for 1–2 minutes, until the paper is crisp, turning so that it is golden brown all over. Drain. Dry on kitchen paper and keep hot. Serve as soon as possible.

small button mushrooms

rice paper

vegetable oil for deep-frying

## A Hallowe'en Feast

Hallowe'en has an extraordinary atmosphere about it, especially when it falls at a weekend. Children bobbing for apples, pumpkin faces on the window-sill with a lit candle inside, 'tricking or treating' – all customs that are generations old, symbolic of purging the old year of devils and making way for All Saints' Day the following morning.

These antics are hungry work, so traditionally I make a little feast every year for my children when their energy is exhausted. I dish up the thick vegetable soup with lots of hot bread and some cheeses, followed by – what else – Devil's Cake.

## Guy Fawkes Toffee Apples

SERVES 6

November 5 comes round again, perhaps the most uniquely British of all our festivals, commemorating as it does the Gunpowder Plot to blow up the Houses of Parliament in 1605. Bonfires are lit all over the country, fulfilling the pagan rite of banishing evil spirits, and firework displays light up the night sky. Children watch wide-eyed, warmly wrapped against the cold – and sustained by these sweet and crunchy toffee apples.

Wash and dry the apples, remove the stalks and push a lolly stick into each one.

To make the toffee, put the sugar and 5 tbls of water into a heavy-bottomed pan and heat gently until the sugar has dissolved, stirring occasionally. Add the butter, golden syrup and lemon juice, and stir until well blended. Turn up the heat and boil rapidly without stirring, until the toffee reaches 145°C/290°F. Remove from the heat and allow the bubbles to subside. Dip in the apples, one at a time, until they are completely covered. Stand on greaseproof paper until set. Cool completely before offering them round.

6 apples

6 wooden lolly sticks

175 g (6 oz) soft brown sugar

25 g (1 oz) butter

50 g (2 oz) golden syrup

½ tsp lemon juice

# Spooky Soup

SERVES 8–10

Sauté the onions in the butter in a large saucepan, stirring until they soften. Cook them for about 10 minutes but be careful not to brown them. Add the pumpkin flesh, turnips and carrots and stir until the vegetables are well coated with the onions. Cook gently for 5 minutes to soften them, then stir in the stock and bring to the boil. Simmer for 15 minutes, then liquidize to a purée. Season to taste with salt, pepper and nutmeg. Stir in the cream. Heat through and the soup is ready to serve.

2 large onions, sliced

50 g (2 oz) butter

500 g (1 lb) pumpkin flesh, chopped

250 g (8 oz) turnips, sliced

350 g (12 oz) carrots, sliced

1.75 l (3 pts) stock (see p. 149)

salt and pepper

ground nutmeg

300 ml (½ pt) double cream

# Devil's Cake

SERVES 10–12

This is simply a sublime chocolate cake: rich, light and very chocolatey. To celebrate Hallowe'en, try decorating it with white icing (just icing sugar and water) in a cobweb design!

Melt the chocolate over a pan of hot water. Stir in 3 tbls of warm water until smooth. Cool a little. Cream the butter with the sugar and beat in the eggs and the melted chocolate. Add the milk alternately with the flour. Add the vanilla essence. Pour into a 20-cm (8-in) cake tin and bake at gas mark 4/180°C/350°F until a knife plunged into the centre comes out clean, about 50 minutes. Leave in the tin for 10 minutes, then turn out to cool on a wire rack. Cut in half and spread with a thin layer of apricot jam.

125 g (4 oz) plain chocolate

175 g (6 oz) butter

300 g (10 oz) dark-brown sugar

3 eggs, beaten

150 ml (¼ pt) milk

250 g (8 oz) self-raising flour

vanilla essence

2–3 tbls apricot jam

# Firelit Suppers

The autumn morning waked by many a gun
Throws o'er the fields her many-coloured light
Wood wildly touched close tanned and stubbled dun
A motley paradise for earth's delight
Clouds ripple as the darkness breaks to light
And clover fields are hid with silver mist
One shower of cobwebs o'er the surface spread
And threads of silk in strange disorder twist
Round every leaf and blossoms bottly head
Hares in the drowning herbage scarcely steal
But on the battered pathway squats abed
And by the cart rut nips her morning meal
Look where we may the scene is strange and new
And every object wears a changing hue

John Clare, *A Autumn Morning*

# Garlicky Aubergine Slices

SERVES 4

On a chilly autumn evening, this snack of garlicky aubergine slices, covered with melted cheese and placed on crisp sesame-coated toasts, is irresistible. It is fireside food, an informal but memorable meal that I love to serve with a mixed salad and a bottle of red wine.

Sprinkle the aubergines with salt and leave them to sweat for 20 minutes. Pat them dry with a kitchen towel.

Mix the garlic into the beaten eggs and dip the aubergine slices into it. Then dip them into the seasoned flour and deep-fry in oil heated to 190°C/375°F until golden all over, about 5 minutes. Drain on kitchen paper. Place each one on a sesame toast (see below), cover with a slice of cheese, and grill until it melts. Serve at once.

*To make the sesame toasts:* Butter the bread thickly. Press the sesame seeds all over the surface. Cut each slice in half. Bake at gas mark 2/150°C/300°F until crisp and golden, about 20 minutes.

2 medium aubergines, cut into 5-mm (¼-in) slices

salt and pepper

1 large clove of garlic, crushed

2 eggs, beaten

50 g (2 oz) wholemeal flour, seasoned

oil for deep-frying

175 g (6 oz) Gruyère cheese, sliced

*For the sesame toasts*

6 slices of bread, crusts removed

butter or margarine

3 tbls sesame seeds

## Noodles with Oriental Vegetables

SERVES 4

This luscious combination of egg noodles and stir-fried vegetables, spiced with ginger and garlic and seasoned with soy sauce, is one of my favourite supper dishes. It is quick and simple to prepare.

Stir-fry the vegetables in a wok or large pan in the sesame oil. When they are well coated and beginning to soften, add the ginger, spring onions and garlic, and stir in thoroughly. Cook for another minute, then add the soy sauce and heat through again. Toss with the cooked noodles and serve immediately.

500 g (1 lb) selection of French beans (cut into 5-mm/$\frac{1}{4}$-in lengths), mange-tout (finely sliced diagonally), tiny button mushrooms (halved), sweetcorn (canned) and Chinese leaf (shredded)

4 tbls sesame oil

2.5-cm (1-in) piece of root ginger, grated

4 spring onions, finely chopped

1 large clove of garlic, finely chopped

1–2 tbls soy sauce

250 g (8 oz) egg noodles, cooked

## Broccoli and Mushroom Gratin

SERVES 4

Simple family fare, this combination of mushrooms and broccoli in a béchamel sauce is topped with a nutty, cheesy oatmeal layer that turns golden in the baking.

Stir the mushrooms into the béchamel sauce and heat through gently. Season to taste. Steam the broccoli florets for 3–4 minutes until softened a little, and put into an ovenproof serving dish. Pour the mushroom sauce over the top.

Combine the oatmeal, nuts and cheese, and season with salt and pepper. Sprinkle this mixture over the top of the vegetables and bake at gas mark 5/190°C/375°F for 15 minutes.

125 g (4 oz) mushrooms, sliced

450 ml ($\frac{3}{4}$ pt) béchamel sauce (see p. 148)

300 g (10 oz) broccoli florets

50 g (2 oz) medium oatmeal

50 g (2 oz) dry-roasted peanuts, very finely chopped

75 g (3 oz) Cheddar cheese, finely grated

# Harvest Pasties

SERVES 4

This variation on the theme of a Cornish pastie makes a nourishing, filling meal, autumnal in flavour with its mixture of root vegetables. It is cosy, family food, perfect for an informal supper around the fire, and needs only a tomato salad to go with it.

Boil the onion for 10 minutes, then cool, peel and chop. Cook the other vegetables together for 10 minutes. Cool and cut into tiny dice. Stir into the béchamel sauce with the onion and chopped parsley and season with salt, pepper and mace. Chill.

Roll the pastry out thinly and cut into 4 × 15-cm (6-in) squares. Pile one quarter of the vegetable mixture into the centre of each one, and fold over to form a triangle. Moisten the edges of the pastry and press together with a fork. Brush with beaten egg and bake at gas mark 7/220°C/425°F for 10 minutes, then at gas mark 4/180°C/ 350°F until crisp and golden, about another 20 minutes.

1 onion

2 medium carrots, sliced

4 medium potatoes

4 small turnips

450 ml (¾ pt) béchamel sauce (see p. 148)

1 small bunch of parsley, chopped

salt and pepper

1–2 tsp ground mace

400 g (14 oz) shortcrust pastry (see p. 148)

1 egg, beaten

*An hour of concentrated work does more to kindle joy, to overcome sadness and set your ship afloat again, than a month of gloomy brooding.*

Ben Franklin

## Seasonal Side Vegetables

*The autumn trees, ravaged as they are, take on the flash of tattered flags kindling in the gloom of cool cathedral caves where gold letters on marble pages describe death in battle and how bones bleach and burn far away in Indian sands. The autumn trees gleam in the yellow moonlight, in the light of harvest moons, the light which mellows the energy of labour, and smooths the stubble, and brings the waves lapping blue to the shore.*

Virginia Woolf, *To the Lighthouse*

# Cauliflower with Cobnuts

SERVES 4

If you can get to the cobnuts before the squirrels, these tasty, milky nuts make a delicious addition to vegetables. Lightly steamed cauliflower, tossed in nut-brown butter and sprinkled with chopped cobs or hazelnuts, is one of autumn's treats.

Steam the cauliflower florets *al dente* and keep warm in a serving dish. Heat the butter until it turns a nut-brown colour and begins to froth. Pour over the cauliflower, sprinkle on the nuts and toss thoroughly. Season with a little sea salt and pepper, and it is ready to serve.

1 cauliflower, broken into florets

50 g (2 oz) butter

40 g (1½ oz) cobnuts, chopped

sea salt and pepper

# Potatoes in Coriander Sauce

SERVES 4

This sauce, based on an oriental recipe, is a good way to use the last of the coriander before its season is over. A touch of turmeric gives it a little heat, which permeates the gently cooking potatoes. A mouth-watering combination.

Pour 300 ml (½ pt) of boiling water over the desiccated coconut and leave to steep for 10 minutes. Blend the peanuts, coriander seeds, turmeric and coriander with the strained coconut milk and stir in the cream. Pour over the potatoes in a saucepan, bring to simmering point and heat gently until cooked through but still slightly crisp, about 6–8 minutes.

1 tbls desiccated coconut

2 tbls dry-roasted peanuts

½ tbls coriander seeds

1 tsp turmeric

2 tbls coriander, chopped

5 tbls thick cream

500 g (1 lb) potatoes, peeled and sliced 5 mm (¼ in) thick

salt to taste

## Beetroot with Cream and Garlic

SERVES 4

Freshly cooked beetroot is one of the finest of vegetables, and makes wonderful autumn food – nourishing, sweet and sustaining. Treated to a cream and garlic sauce, it is gastronomic.

Boil the beetroots in their skins until tender, about 15–20 minutes. Cool a little and skin them. Cut into small cubes and put into a serving dish. Keep warm. Heat the cream gently and stir in the garlic for about 3–4 minutes, making sure that the cream does not boil. Season liberally with freshly ground pepper and pour over the beetroot.

750 g (1½ lb) beetroot, washed and trimmed

300 ml (½ pt) single cream

2 cloves of garlic, crushed

freshly ground pepper

## Spiced Cauliflower

SERVES 4

As the days grow chillier, a touch of Indian spicing in food can be pleasantly warming. The spices used in this dish give life to the bland delicacy of cauliflower. I like to serve it with pasta, and also with the Garlicky Aubergine Slices on p. 71.

Fry the desiccated coconut and sesame seeds in the combined oils until brown. Add the garam masala and stir well. Thin out with a little water, put the cauliflower florets into the pan and toss until well coated. Add 4–5 tbls more water and steam, covered with a lid, until the cauliflower is tender, about 5–8 minutes.

1 tbls desiccated coconut

15 g (½ oz) sesame seeds

2 tbls sesame oil

1 tbls sunflower oil

2–3 tsps garam masala

1 cauliflower, broken into florets

salt to taste

# Autumnal Treats

So thick a mist hung over all,
Rain had no room to fall;
It seemed a sea without a shore;
The cobwebs drooped heavy and hoar
As though with wool they had been knit;
Too obvious mark for fly to hit!

And though the sun was somewhere else
The gloom had brightness of its own
That shone on bracken, grass and stone
And mole-mound with its broken shells
That told where squirrel lately sat,
Cracked hazel-nuts and ate the fat.

And sullen haws in the hedgerows
Burned in the damp with clearer fire;
And brighter still than those
The scarlet hips hung on the briar
Like coffins of the dead dog-rose;
All were as bright as though for earth
Death were a gayer thing than birth.

Andrew Young, *Autumn Mist*

## Blackberry Sorbet

SERVES 6

There are countless traditional ways of using the prolific crop of blackberries that festoon our hedgerows every autumn: crumbles, pies, jams, fools and tarts, to name but some. This sorbet does full justice to a fine fruit – it is an exquisite dessert. And it keeps in the freezer for several months, so that we can re-live the taste of autumn when winter is fully upon us.

Cook the blackberries in a few tablespoons of water until they are completely soft and all the juices have run. Cool and strain, reserving the juice. Heat with the sugar in a heavy-bottomed pan and bring to the boil. Simmer for 5–6 minutes, until it forms a light syrup. Cool.

Liquidize this juice with the peaches and pour into a container. Freeze. Stir after 1 hour and then leave to freeze completely for at least 6 hours.

500 g (1 lb) blackberries, washed

125 g (4 oz) sugar

400-g (14-oz) can of peaches, drained

*Your joy is your sorrow unmasked. And the self same well from which your laughter rises was oftentimes filled with your tears.*

Kahlil Gibran, *The Prophet*

# Bilberry Drop Scones

MAKES 12

If you live too far south in England to gather bilberries from the wild, you can now buy them from certain supermarkets. A beautiful colour – deep blue with a dusky bloom on them – bilberries are lusciously tasty, too.

Sift the flour with the salt and raising agents, and stir in the sugar. Beat the eggs and add to the milk with the warmed syrup. Make a well in the centre of the flour and pour in the liquid mixture. Add the bilberries and mix to a smooth batter.

Put 1 tbls of the mixture at a time on to a hot, well-greased frying pan and cook until golden, about 2 minutes each side. Serve hot, with butter or thick cream.

250 g (8 oz) plain flour

½ tsp salt

2 tsp cream of tartar

1 tsp bicarbonate of soda

25 g (1 oz) caster sugar

2 eggs

225 ml (8 fl oz) milk

1 tbls golden syrup, warmed

175 g (6 oz) ripe bilberries

# Tarte Tatin aux Prunes

SERVES 6

A French friend of mine makes the classic upside-down apple tart, *tarte tatin*, to perfection, and was kind enough to give me her recipe. One year I adapted it so that I could use up a huge crop of plums, and it worked beautifully. So here it is.

Cook the chopped plums in the butter for 2–3 minutes, add sugar to taste and stir over a gentle heat until it dissolves. Put a little malt extract into the bottom of a 25-cm (10-in) flan tin, and add the rest to the plum mixture. Put this into the flan tin and cover with the pastry rolled out to fit over the top with a margin of an extra cm (½ in). Press down with a fork and bake in a pre-heated oven at gas mark 5/190°C/395°F for 45 minutes. Leave to stand for 5–10 minutes, then turn upside-down on to a platter. Serve warm or cold.

1 kg (2 lb) ripe plums, stoned and chopped

75 g (3 oz) butter

sugar to taste

2 tbls malt extract

200 g (7 oz) shortcrust pastry (see p. 149)

# Fuller's-style Walnut Cake

SERVES 10–12

This is undeniably one of the best cakes in the world. It is based on a cake I remember from my Cambridge childhood: Fuller's walnut cake from Fitzbillies, which was a rare treat, a delicacy with its crisp white icing. Making it with the autumn crop of wet walnuts is almost an improvement – if that be possible – on the original, because of the yummy flavour of the walnuts. Delicious with Earl Grey tea.

Sift the flour with the baking powder. Cream the butter with the sugar, then beat in the eggs, one at a time, until the mixture is fluffy. Fold in the flour and add the chopped walnuts. Mix well.

Bake in a greased 20-cm (8-in) cake tin with a removable base at gas mark 3/ 170°C/325°F for 30–40 minutes. Cool for 10 minutes on a rack, then remove from the tin and allow to cool completely before icing.

*To make the icing:* Cream the butter with the icing sugar and add strong coffee until the mixture reaches spreading consistency.

200 g (7 oz) plain flour

1 tsp baking powder

200 g (7 oz) unsalted butter

200 g (7 oz) caster sugar

3 large eggs

50 g (2 oz) walnuts, chopped

*For the icing*

75 g (3 oz) butter or margarine

125 g (4 oz) icing sugar

a little strong coffee

# Pear and Blackberry Flan

SERVES 6

I have a small pear tree in my garden that bears a modest crop of the most delicious fruit – it has a short season, but we make the most of it. One year, coming home after gathering blackberries along the quiet, foggy lanes, it occurred to me to combine the berries with pears instead of apples, just for a change. The result was this flan, voted the best autumn dessert by my family!

Sift the flour with the sugar and rub in the margarine. Mix to a light paste, knead and roll out. Line a 20-cm (8-in) flan tin with two thirds of the pastry.

Slice the pears, mix with the blackberries and put into the lined flan tin. Beat the egg with the sugar until thick, then stir in the flour and beat again. Add the orange rind and juice, and stir until smooth. Pour over the fruit. Bake at gas mark 6/200°C/400°F for 35–40 minutes. Cool and eat warm or cold.

175 g (6 oz) plain flour

25 g (1 oz) icing sugar

75 g (3 oz) margarine

500 g (1 lb) ripe pears, peeled and cored

175 g (6 oz) blackberries

1 egg, beaten

75 g (3 oz) caster sugar

1 tbls plain flour

grated rind and juice of 1 orange

*Serenity is the secret of beauty and the real substance of all art.*

Hermann Hesse

*Winter*

# Winter

# Warming Breakfasts

So in December sing I, while they come
Weary and dull and silent, tramping home
Through rainy dark, the cowman taking down
The hurricane lantern from its usual peg,
And going round the cattle in the stalls,
The shifting, munching cattle in the dark
And aromatic stalls beneath the rafters,
Swinging the lantern as he goes his rounds.
Clapping the kine upon their bony rumps
And seeing to their comfort ere he comes
Back to the ruddy kitchen for his food . . .

V. Sackville-West, *The Land*

# Hot Mushroom Loaf

SERVES 4–6

Succulent and satisfying, these layers of warmed buttered bread and sautéed mushrooms are an unforgettable breakfast on a crisp, cold winter's morning. It's a good brunch, too: served with a poached egg and some grilled tomatoes, it makes a hearty meal that will set you up for a good part of the day.

Cut the crusts off the loaf and slice it into 5 thick lengthwise slices. Butter all the surfaces lightly. Sauté the mushrooms in the rest of the butter for several minutes until soft, and lift out of the pan. Sandwich the layers of bread with the hot mushrooms and wrap in foil. Bake at gas mark 7/220°C/425°F for 20 minutes, then cut it vertically into thick slices. Serve at once on hot plates.

1 large granary loaf

175 g (6 oz) butter

750 g (1½ lb) flat mushrooms, thickly sliced

# Stammer Max

SERVES 2

I had this dish for breakfast on a skiing holiday years ago, and I've never forgotten it. My appetite was sharpened by that wonderfully incisive, clear cold that you get in the mountains, and it was more than satisfied by this mixture of fried bread, smoked haddock and cheese, topped with egg and tomatoes. Yummy, downed with excellent Continental coffee.

Cut the smoked haddock into slices and place on each piece of fried bread. Cover with the sliced cheese. Grill under a hot grill until the cheese bubbles. Fry the eggs in more light oil and grill the tomatoes. Serve topped with the egg and surrounded by the tomatoes.

2 thick smoked haddock fillets

2 slices of bread, fried in light oil

50 g (2 oz) Cheddar cheese, sliced

2 eggs

4 tomatoes

## Fish Turnover

SERVES 2–3

A light pastry parcel filled with a simple mixture of kipper and hard-boiled egg makes a truly wonderful breakfast on a cold morning. It is a welcome change from the conventional bacon-and-eggs type of English breakfast, or just kipper on its own, and is delicious served with grilled tomatoes and a jug of freshly made coffee.

Mash the hard-boiled eggs with the seasonings and stir in the flaked kipper and the chopped parsley (you can prepare this the night before). While the oven is heating, roll out the pastry into a large rectangle, spread the mixture over half of it and fold it over. Seal the edges by moistening them and pressing them together with a fork, and make diagonal cuts across the pastry. Brush with beaten egg. Bake at gas mark 4/180°C/350°F until golden brown, about 20–25 minutes. Cut into slices and serve on warm plates.

2 hard-boiled eggs

salt and pepper

lemon juice

175 g (6 oz) kipper fillet, flaked

2 tbls parsley, chopped

200 g (7 oz) puff pastry

1 egg, beaten

## Grilled Apricot Grapefruit

SERVES 4

Instead of just sprinkling a layer of sugar over the top of your grapefruit, try spreading it lightly with apricot jam and putting it under the grill until it bubbles. A deliciously different way to start the day.

Cut the grapefruit in half and loosen the segments with a serrated knife. Spread lightly with apricot jam and sprinkle demerara sugar over the top. Put under a hot grill for 3–4 minutes until bubbling.

2 large grapefruit

apricot jam

demerara sugar

## Baking Powder Puffs

MAKES 12–15

The smell that wafts out of the kitchen while these lovely light morsels are cooking really gets the mouth watering. By the time I put them on the table with butter, jam and honey, there is no stopping my hungry family: they disappear like the thawing snow!

Sift the dry ingredients together and lightly rub in the margarine. Stir in the milk quickly and knead until light. Roll out on a floured board to 1.5 cm ($\frac{3}{4}$ in) thick, and cut into circles with a cutter or wine glass. Bake at gas mark 8/230°C/450°F until risen and golden brown on top, about 10–15 minutes. Cool on a rack for a few minutes before serving.

250 g (8 oz) plain flour

4 tsps baking powder

1 tsp salt

25 g (1 oz) margarine

200 ml (6 fl oz) milk

## Egg Roll Surprise

SERVES 2

This 'surprise' is a kind of English breakfast in disguise: individual omelettes filled with all kinds of breakfast goodies, rolled up and sliced just before serving. This dish is such a cheering start to our long cold days of winter, which seem to drag on interminably. Consolation food!

Beat the eggs with the milk and season to taste. Make two flat omelettes with the mixture. Put to one side and keep warm.

Sauté the mushrooms in the butter and add the chopped tomato. Toss together until hot and fold in the croûtons. Put half of the mixture on to each omelette and roll up tightly. Cut into slices and serve immediately with croissants and hot coffee or tea.

4 eggs

a little milk

salt and pepper

125 g (4 oz) mushrooms

25 g (1 oz) butter

2 tomatoes, finely chopped

croûtons

# Slimming Foods

I saw how rows of white raindrops
From bare boughs shone,
And how the storm had stript the leaves
Forgetting none
Save one left high on a top twig
Swinging alone;
Then that too bursting into song
Fled and was gone.

Andrew Young, *The Last Leaf*

# Cucumber and Grapefruit Soup with Mint

SERVES 4

I have always felt that winter is a good time to get in trim. Exercise is warming and makes you feel more cheerful, and you can dream of lying on the beach on your summer holiday with the waistline in perfect shape ... This refreshing soup has almost no calories in it, and is simply delicious.

Put the cucumber, grapefruit and stock into the food processor and blend. Chill. Serve in small bowls garnished with the chopped mint.

1 cucumber, peeled and grated

175 g (6 oz) grapefruit segments

300 ml ($\frac{1}{2}$ pt) stock (see p. 149)

*Garnish*

mint, chopped

# Carrot and Orange Soup

SERVES 6

Soups make excellent slimming food if you use low-fat ingredients with the vegetables. This combination of carrot and orange is filling and nourishing – a slimmer's meal in itself.

Simmer the sliced onions in the margarine for 10 minutes over a very gentle heat, covered, until they are well softened. Add the carrots and toss them until well coated, and cook gently for a further 2–3 minutes. Pour the stock over them, bring to boiling point and simmer for 10 minutes, covered. Add the orange rind and simmer for a further 10 minutes. Liquidize to a smooth purée, add the orange juice and the milk and heat through gently until ready to serve.

3 medium onions, thinly sliced

40 g (1$\frac{1}{2}$ oz) sunflower margarine

500 g (1 lb) carrots, sliced

600 ml (1 pt) stock (see p. 149)

grated rind and juice of 1 orange

150 ml ($\frac{1}{4}$ pt) skimmed milk

# Raw Mushrooms with Spicy Sauce

SERVES 4

This is an extraordinarily delicious salad, original and mouth-wateringly tasty, and so simple to prepare. The mayonnaise is exotically spiced with garam masala, tahini, and with more than a hint of garlic to stimulate the taste-buds!

Mix the garam masala with the mayonnaise and stir in the tahini. Add the crushed garlic and leave to stand for half an hour, so that the flavours can mingle. Dress the sliced mushrooms with the spiced mayonnaise, toss thoroughly and sprinkle with the chopped coriander.

1–2 tsp garam masala

150 ml ($\frac{1}{4}$ pt) mayonnaise (see p. 148)

2 tbls tahini paste

1 large clove of garlic, crushed

350 g (12 oz) button mushrooms, very thinly sliced

*Garnish*

coriander, chopped

# Chinese Leaf Rolls

SERVES 4

A friend of mine, who is a wizard with 'raw food', introduced me to this idea, so the credit goes to Dawn for this recipe! It's a delightful dish: fresh and light, yet satisfying. I like to serve it with winter cole-slaw. The whole meal is so delicious that you quite forget that it is 'slimming food'!

Separate the leaves of the cabbage and steam them for 2 minutes, until they are soft and supple. Mix the cottage cheese with the yogurt. Cut the Brie into small cubes. Squeeze the grated cucumber in a towel until it is dry. Mix the Brie and cucumber into the cottage cheese mixture with the chopped celery and dill, and stir thoroughly. Season to taste with pepper. Put tablespoons of the mixture into the middle of each cabbage leaf and roll up, tucking in the ends like a parcel. Place in a serving dish and chill until ready to eat.

1 Chinese cabbage

350 g (12 oz) cottage cheese, puréed

5 tbls natural-set yogurt

125 g (4 oz) Brie, skinned

1 cucumber, grated

1 celery heart, chopped in small pieces

1 bunch of dill, finely chopped

freshly ground black pepper

# Yogurt Shake with Fresh Fruit

SERVES 4

Here is a permissible dessert for slimmers!
Light, refreshing, healthy food that will
not infringe the regime! The sugar is
optional, since the natural sugars in the
fruits are sufficient sweetening for most
people.

Liquidize the yogurt with the cottage
cheese and then stir in all the fruits.
Sweeten to taste and chill.

3 large tbls yogurt

175 g (6 oz) cottage
cheese

2 satsumas, peeled and
divided into segments

75 g (3 oz) pineapple,
cut into small cubes

1 banana, sliced

1 tbls mixed peel,
chopped

icing sugar to taste
(optional)

*Even the severed branch grows again, and the sunken moon
returns; wise men who ponder this are not troubled in
adversity.*

Bharthari

93

# A Winter Dinner Party

Now stir the fire, and close the shutters fast,
Let fall the curtains, wheel the sofa round,
And, while the bubbling and loud-hissing urn
Throws up a steamy column, and the cups,
That cheer but not inebriate, wait on each,
So let us welcome peaceful evening in...

William Cowper, *The Task*

The Menu

Poireaux Vinaigrette aux Noix

Fettuccine with Mozzarella and Sweet
Peppers

Spinach Bourekakia with Fennel Salad

Nègre en Chemise

I give most of my dinner parties in the winter. I really enjoy those cosy
afternoons in the kitchen preparing a wonderful meal, as a blizzard rages
outside, or the grey mists of February descend. Leeks often feature on the
menu – the most gastronomic of our winter vegetables, in my view – and
likewise freshly cut spinach. I have served this menu to an enthusiastic
response more than once, with small helpings of each course so as not to
overload either the taste-buds or the stomach. The pudding, as a finale, is
a *tour de force*.

# Poireaux Vinaigrette aux Noix

**SERVES 6**

Young, tender leeks, simply dressed in
walnut oil and tossed with chopped
walnuts and parsley, make a mouth-
watering starter. They can be prepared
well in advance, too, which is a major
advantage, and need just fresh granary
bread as an accompaniment.

Steam the leeks until completely soft,
about 10–15 minutes. Allow them to
cool. Sprinkle with the chopped walnuts
and parsley. Spoon walnut oil over the top
and toss thoroughly. Season with a little
sea salt. Arrange in a pretty dish and serve
at room temperature.

1 kg (2 lb) small leeks,
washed and trimmed

75 g (3 oz) walnuts,
finely chopped

1 small bunch of
parsley, finely chopped

6–8 tbls walnut oil

sea salt

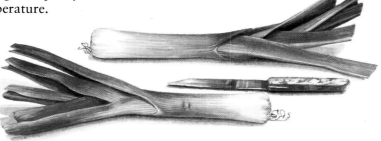

## Fettucine, Mozzarella and Sweet Peppers

SERVES 6

A small pasta course, served after a little gap in the proceedings, is an unusual but popular idea, I find. The delicacy of mozzarella, the sweet spiciness of yellow peppers and a touch of garlic are the features of this dish.

Grill the peppers, skin-side up, until they are soft, peel off the skin, and chop finely. Mix the olive oil with the crushed garlic and fold into the hot, drained fettucine. Toss in the mozzarella and peppers, season to taste with a little salt, and keep hot until ready to serve.

2 yellow peppers, cut in half and de-seeded

5 tbls olive oil

2 cloves of garlic, crushed

500 g (1 lb) fettuccine, cooked *al dente*

125 g (4 oz) mozzarella, cut into little strips

salt to taste

## Spinach Bourekakia with Fennel Salad

SERVES 6

Filo pastry is now widely available – and it is easy to use, and so rewarding. It makes these light, crisp, golden morsels filled with a creamy mixture of spinach and feta cheese, which are perfectly balanced by the citrusy, sensational, fennel salad – for which thanks go to my friend Barbara, who gave it to me for lunch one day. It made such an impression that I had to include it!

Mix all the filling ingredients together. Put a heaped tablespoon of the mixture into the centre of a sheet of filo pastry and roll it up, tucking in the ends as you go to make a neat parcel. Brush with olive oil and bake at gas mark 6/200°C/400°F until golden brown, about 15 minutes.

18 sheets of filo pastry, each measuring 15 cm (6 in) square

3 tbls olive oil

*For the filling*

500 g (1 lb) spinach, cooked, drained and chopped

175 g (6 oz) feta or goat cheese, crumbled

125 g (4 oz) cottage cheese

2 eggs, lightly beaten

6 spring onions, finely chopped

2–3 tbls mint, chopped

freshly ground black pepper

*To make the fennel salad:* Simmer the sliced lemon rind for 5 minutes. Drain. Cut the pith off the lemon and slice the fruit finely, then cut the slices in half. Mix together the fennel, rind, fruit of the lemon, and the parsley. Dress with the vinaigrette into which you have stirred a little cream. Season with black pepper and toss again.

**For the fennel salad**

1 lemon, the rind pared and very finely sliced

2 heads of fennel, blanched and finely sliced

1 small bunch of parsley, finely chopped

3 tbls vinaigrette

a little single cream

# Nègre en Chemise

SERVES 6

A classic pudding. This is rich, luscious food with the delectable combination of chocolate and kirsch – all smothered with a layer of whipped cream. But serve it in modest portions, because a little goes a long way!

Melt the chocolate with a little black coffee in a bowl over hot water. Cream the icing sugar (reserving a little for later) with the butter and stir in the melted chocolate. Mix in the egg yolks and one glass of the kirsch. Whisk the egg whites until stiff and fold into the mixture.

Butter a 17.5-cm (7-in) × 10-cm (4-in) mould. Line the bottom with the biscuits dipped into a little kirsch mixed with an equal quantity of water. Put a layer of the chocolate mixture over the biscuits, then another layer of the biscuits, and so on. Chill. Turn out and cover with whipped cream beaten with a little icing sugar.

175 g (6 oz) plain chocolate

a little black coffee

125 g (4 oz) icing sugar

150 g (5 oz) butter

3 eggs, separated

3 wine glasses of kirsch

300 g (10 oz) boudoir biscuits

150 ml ($\frac{1}{4}$ pt) double cream

*Garnish*
icing sugar

# Celebrating Winter Festivals

O for a pleasant book to cheat the sway
Of winter – where rich mirth with hearty laugh
Listens and rubs his legs on corner seat
For fields are mire and sludge – and badly off
Are those who on their pudgy paths delay
There striding shepherd seeking driest way
Fearing nights wetshod feet and hacking cough
That keeps him waken till the peep of day
Goes shouldering onward and with ready hook
Progs oft to ford the sloughs that nearly meet
Across the lands – croodling and thin to view
His loath dog follows – stops and quakes and looks
For better roads – till whistled to pursue
Then on with frequent jump he hirkles through

John Clare, *Winter Fields*

# Yule Log

SERVES 8

Christmas can be so overdone, and many people dread the razzmatazz associated with it. For me, one of the things that helps make Christmas gentler and less commercial is the making of my own home-made specialities. Lots of them can be prepared well in advance, so this isn't as gruelling as it might sound! And, anyway, this yule log is unbelievably good – you couldn't buy it anywhere if you tried!

Cream the butter with half of the sugar. Add the egg yolks and beat thoroughly. Whisk the whites until stiff, fold in the rest of the sugar and beat again. Fold the whites into the butter–sugar mixture alternately with the flour, fruit, chocolate and nuts. Bake in a 500-g (1-lb) loaf tin at gas mark 4/180°C/350°F until a knife comes out clean from the centre, about 1 hour. Cool on a rack and remove from the tin when cold. Cut into two halves down the middle, and join up to form one long log. Cover with the chocolate cream (below) and stud the top with Christmas decorations – the robin, the fir tree and the other plastic paraphernalia that emerge every year from the depths of your cupboard to delight the children...

*To make the chocolate cream:* Melt the chocolate with 3 tbls of water in a bowl over hot water. Remove from the heat and beat in the egg yolks. Whip the cream until quite stiff and fold it into the chocolate mixture, with icing sugar to taste. Add the liqueur if using. Chill.

125 g (4 oz) butter or margarine

125 g (4 oz) caster sugar

2 eggs, separated

125 g (4 oz) plain flour, sifted

50 g (2 oz) raisins

50 g (2 oz) candied peel, or cherries, or both

50 g (2 oz) plain chocolate, chopped

250 g (8 oz) mixed nuts, chopped

*For the chocolate cream*

75 g (3 oz) chocolate

2 egg yolks

300 ml ($\frac{1}{2}$ pt) double cream

icing sugar to taste

rum or kirsch to taste (optional)

## Best Christmas Cake

### SERVES 12 OR MORE

I have been making this cake for years now, simply because I have never tasted a better one. Try it: it is sensational. You can make it well in advance of those busy weeks just before the big day, since it actually improves on keeping. It also freezes very well, so if some is left over you can store it for a future occasion.

Divide the flour into three bowls. Add the fruit and nuts to one bowl and mix thoroughly. Sift all the spices, the baking powder and the salt into the second bowl. Cream the butter with the sugar, and beat the eggs into this mixture alternately with the spiced flour. Beat very thoroughly. Add the fruit and flour mixture, mix well and then fold in the third bowl of flour. Stir thoroughly and add the brandy or stout. Line a 1-kg (2-lb) loaf tin with three layers of greaseproof paper and put the cake mixture in, and smooth it down with the back of a spoon. Bake at gas mark 2/ 150°C/300°F for 2 hours. Keep in the tin until cold, then store, well wrapped in cling-film, for as long as possible.

250 g (8 oz) plain flour, sifted

500 g (1 lb) currants

500 g (1 lb) seeded raisins

250 g (8 oz) glacé cherries, chopped

125 g (4 oz) mixed peel, chopped

125 g (4 oz) Jordan almonds, skinned and chopped

1 tsp ground mixed spice

1 tsp ground ginger

1 tsp ground cinnamon

1 tsp ground nutmeg

1 tsp baking powder

a tiny pinch of salt

250 g (8 oz) butter

250 g (8 oz) sugar

6 eggs

5 tbls brandy (or stout works quite well)

# Christmas Pudding Special

SERVES 8–10

Lots of people I know really don't much like the traditional steamed Christmas pudding. So if your family isn't keen, try this idea on them. It is a puréed mixture of fruits and nuts and fruit juice, packed down and chilled (and it freezes very well if you want to make it in advance). It is wonderful with the Brandy and Ginger Ice-cream below.

Mix all the ingredients together and put half at a time into the food processor. Blend to a rough purée. Pack into a pudding basin and press down well. Chill for at least 24 hours.

To serve, decorate with sifted icing sugar, slivered browned almonds and holly.

250 g (8 oz) raisins

250 g (8 oz) dates

2 fresh bananas

2 dried bananas

125 g (4 oz) cashew nuts

50 g (2 oz) dried apricots, chopped in small pieces

juice of 1 lemon

*Garnish*

icing sugar

slivered almonds, toasted

holly

# Brandy and Ginger Ice-cream

SERVES 6

Epicurean is not an exaggeration for this ice-cream – indeed, it is the only fitting adjective. Ginger is my favourite spice, and this lovely light ice-cream, laced with brandy, makes one of the best of all the Christmas treats.

Sift the icing sugar with the ginger and fold into the cream with the brandy. Beat until stiff. Fold in the stiffly beaten egg whites and freeze until nearly set, about 1–2 hours. Fold in the stem ginger and freeze again until set. Allow to soften slightly and serve in scoops, decorated with the chopped stem ginger.

125 g (4 oz) icing sugar

1–2 tsps ground ginger

300 ml ($\frac{1}{2}$ pt) double cream

2–3 tbls brandy

4 egg whites, stiffly beaten

4–6 large pieces of stem ginger, chopped in very small pieces

*Garnish*

stem ginger, chopped in very small pieces

# New Year Supper Parties

*Time, like an aged gardener,*
*Still tends the garden of the year,*
*And, when the summer sweets are lost,*
*He weaves the scentless flowers of frost.*

*When, too, the forest boughs have shed*
*Their generation of the dead,*
*Against the stars the sacred trees*
*Spread out their naked traceries.*

*And in the night an amorous moon*
*Sings to the sea a tender tune,*
*And all the star-encrusted sky*
*Shivers with silent ecstasy.*

*For Beauty thus not only glows*
*Within the wine-cup of the rose,*
*But like a hermit clad may be*
*In garment of austerity.*

Andrew Young, *Winter*

transfer to a wire rack to cool completely.
To make the icing, sift the icing sugar into a large
bowl with the grated orange zest. Gradually add the
juice until smooth, thick 'ribbons' form. Drizzle over
the cooled cake.

## Sticky Ginger and Orange Cake

Takes 1 hr 15 mins to prepare and cook.

125g unsalted butter
125g black treacle
125g golden syrup
150ml milk
125g dark muscovado sugar
225g plain flour
4 tsp ground ginger
1/2 tsp bicarbonate of soda
2 eggs, lightly beaten
2 balls of stem ginger chopped

Icing - 100g icing sugar
          juice and finely grated zest of 1 orange

Pre-heat oven to 180c/Gas 4. Grease and line 20cm square tin.

Place butter, treacle, syrup, milk and sugar in a saucepan. Heat gently, stirring, for 10 mins, or until melted. Remove from the heat.

In a large bowl, sift together the flour, ground ginger and bicarbonate of soda. Add the treacle mixture and fold together. Add the beaten eggs and stem ginger and mix well.

Pour the batter into the prepare tin and knock the tin against a work surface a couple of times to release any air bubbles. Bake in the tin for 45 mins or until

# Sticky Ginger and Orange Cake

Takes 1 hr 15 mins to prepare and cook

The Menus

<table>
<tr><td>Menu 1</td><td>Stilton and Onion Soup Gratinée<br>Chinese-style Cod<br>Snowballs</td></tr>
<tr><td>Menu 2</td><td>Leeks filled with Avocado Purée<br>Fish Crumble<br>Pears with Praline</td></tr>
</table>

Here I am at my dinner parties again – but it has always struck me that they are one of the most pleasant ways of spending those bitter dreary evenings, of fending off the cold and forgetting the greyness. I have devised two menus with cold weather in mind – warming, nourishing food, yet not heavy – just delicious meals to enjoy with good company.

*Menu 1*

# Stilton and Onion Soup Gratinée

### SERVES 4

Alas the leftover Stilton, is the subdued cry from many a household in early January. Here's an answer to some of it: one of the best soups in the world.

Cook the sliced onion in the oil very gently, covered, turning from time to time, until soft and sweet, about 20–25 minutes. Season with salt and add the stock. Simmer for 5–10 minutes, adjust the seasoning and pour into 4 ovenproof soup dishes. Sprinkle the Stilton over the top and put under a very hot grill until the cheese melts and bubbles. Serve with hot French bread.

4 large Spanish onions, thinly sliced

3 tbls vegetable oil

sea salt

900 ml (1½ pts) vegetable stock

250 g (8 oz) Stilton, finely crumbled

## Chinese-style Cod

SERVES 4

Fresh cod is at its very best during the very worst of our winter weather. I pity the fishermen, but I appreciate the results of their labours! A real party-piece.

Season the fish cutlets with salt and pepper, and cover each one with some chopped coriander. Wrap in food-wrap and steam for 6–8 minutes until cooked through.

Combine the remaining ingredients and simmer them together, with a little water if necessary, for 2 minutes. Unwrap the cutlets, remove the coriander, and serve with the black bean sauce spooned over the top of each one.

4 cod cutlets

salt and pepper

1 small bunch of coriander, chopped

4 tbls fermented black beans

1 tbls soy sauce

2 tbls oyster sauce

2.5-cm (1-in) piece of root ginger, grated

1 small clove of garlic, crushed

2 spring onions, finely sliced

## Snowballs

SERVES 4

I found this recipe in an ancient notebook that my mother kept when we lived in one of the Cambridge colleges. I nearly passed over it because it looked unreal: I didn't believe that it could work. But it is a sensational, elegant dessert, rather like *œufs à la neige*.

Cream the butter with the sugar. Add the milk and vanilla and beat again. Fold in the egg whites, and then the flour sifted with the raising agents. Put the mixture into 8 well-buttered individual *timbale* moulds and place in a dish of hot water. Bake at gas mark 4/180°C/350°F for 20 minutes and allow to cool on a rack for 3–4 minutes. Remove carefully from the moulds and cool completely.

To serve, float them in the *crème anglaise* with a little sifted icing sugar over the top.

50 g (2 oz) butter

125 g (4 oz) icing sugar

4 tbls milk

vanilla essence

2 egg whites, very stiffly beaten

50 g (2 oz) plain flour

1 tsp baking powder

$\frac{1}{4}$ tsp salt

600 ml (1 pt) *crème anglaise* (see p. 149)

*MENU 2*

## Leeks Filled with Avocado Purée

**SERVES 4**

A starter of cold leeks filled with a tasty avocado purée and garnished with coriander leaves gets a winter dinner party off to an excellent start. I like to serve this with melba toast (see p. 148) and a good white Burgundy.

Steam the leeks until tender, about 12–15 minutes, then allow them to cool. Cut in half lengthwise and scoop out along the middle to make a hollow. Reserve this tender centre part of the leek for a quiche or soup.

Purée the avocado flesh with the lemon juice, rind, garlic and yogurt. Season with salt and pepper. Fill the hollowed-out leeks with the mixture, and chill. Just before serving, garnish with coriander leaves.

8 large leeks, washed and trimmed

flesh of 2 ripe avocados

rind and juice of $\frac{1}{2}$ lemon

1 clove of garlic, crushed

250 g (8 oz) Greek yogurt

salt and pepper

*Garnish*
coriander leaves

# Fish Crumble

### SERVES 4

Simple though this may seem, it is a warming, aromatic and nourishing main course. Serve it with steamed vegetables of your choice, and a crisp salad to follow.

Wrap the fish in food-wrap and steam until lightly cooked, about 6–8 minutes. Cool, then remove the skin and bones and flake the fish. Mix with the shellfish. Quarter the mushrooms and mix into the béchamel sauce with the chopped fennel leaves, then fold into the fish. Season to taste and put into a soufflé dish.

Crumble the butter into the flour until it resembles fine breadcrumbs. Stir in the Parmesan. Sprinkle over the fish mixture and cook at gas mark 5/190°C/375°F until browned, about 20–25 minutes.

350 g (12 oz) mackerel

350 g (12 oz) coley

100 g (4 oz) prawns, cooked

100 g (4 oz) mussels, cooked

175 g (6 oz) small button mushrooms, steamed

300 ml ($\frac{1}{2}$ pt) béchamel sauce (see p. 148)

2 tbls fennel leaves, finely chopped

salt and pepper

75 g (3 oz) butter or margarine

175 g (6 oz) plain flour, sifted

2 tbls Parmesan cheese, grated

# Pears with Praline

SERVES 4

Ever since I discovered how to make praline, I have thought it the most delicious thing in the world. These lightly poached pears flavoured with vanilla and sprinkled with praline are an incomparable dessert.

Make a light syrup with 450 ml ($\frac{3}{4}$ pt) of water and the sugar by gently heating together for 5 minutes. Poach the pears in the syrup for 4–5 minutes, turning them, then drain and cool. Chill.

Place in shallow glass dishes and sprinkle with the praline just before serving.

*To make the praline:* Put the almonds and sugar into a heavy saucepan over a low heat, until the sugar dissolves. Cook to a rich-brown colour. Pour on to a well-oiled baking sheet, spreading the almonds so that they form a single layer. Leave to cool, then break up and crush with a rolling pin, or break up in the food processor. Store in an air-tight jar.

50 g (2 oz) sugar

4 pears, peeled, cored and quartered

vanilla essence to taste

*For the praline*

125 g (4 oz) almonds

125 g (4 oz) sugar

# Seasonal Side Vegetables

The Frost performs its secret ministry,
Unhelped by any wind. The owlet's cry
Came loud – and hark, again! loud as before.
The inmates of my cottage, all at rest,
Have left me to that solitude, which suits
Abstruser musings: save that at my side
My cradled infant slumbers peacefully.

. . .

Therefore all seasons shall be sweet to thee,
Whether the summer clothe the general earth
With greenness, or the redbreast sit and sing
Betwixt the tufts of snow on the bare branch
Of mossy apple-tree, while the nigh thatch
Smokes in the sun-thaw; whether the eave-drops fall
Heard only in the trances of the blast,
Or if the secret ministry of frost
Shall hang them up in silent icicles,
Quietly shining to the quiet Moon.

Samuel Taylor Coleridge, *Frost at Midnight*

# Cabbage Paysanne

SERVES 6–8

Full of hearty country tastes, this recipe is vaguely Mediterranean in character: layers of cabbage, leeks and tomatoes, with olives on top. Delicious with baked fish or a simple pasta dish.

Steam the cabbage and leeks separately. Make layers with the cabbage, leeks and tomatoes in a baking dish, seasoning as you go. Cover tightly with foil and a lid. Heat through at gas mark 6/200°C/400°F for 10 minutes. Finally, toss in the olives and cubed cheese and it is ready to serve.

1 medium white cabbage, finely sliced

3 medium leeks, sliced

400-g (14-oz) can of tomatoes, drained and sliced

salt and pepper

75 g (3 oz) black olives, stoned and halved

50 g (2 oz) hard cheese, cut into small cubes

# Jerusalem Artichokes with Browned Almonds

SERVES 4

The earthy, nutty taste of Jerusalem artichokes is delicate and quite uniquely conjures winter – I love them! Here their flavour is enhanced by garlic and parsley, and the garnish of browned almonds is delectable.

Cook the artichokes in boiling water until tender but not mushy, about 7–8 minutes. Cool, then slice them thickly. Melt the butter in a large pan and toss the artichokes in it until well coated. Stir in the garlic and parsley and cook, stirring, for 3–4 minutes over a gentle heat. Put into a warmed serving dish and keep warm. Brown the slivered almonds under the grill and scatter them over the top just before serving.

500 g (1 lb) Jerusalem artichokes, peeled

40 g (1½ oz) butter

1 large clove of garlic, crushed

1 small bunch of parsley, finely chopped

*Garnish*

25 g (1 oz) slivered almonds, toasted

# Stir-fry Leeks with Mushrooms

SERVES 4

Stir-fried leeks are a revelation in taste – they are wonderful. Here, with a few mushrooms and a little soy sauce, the touch of Chinese influence brings out the best in them.

Cut the leeks into 7.5-cm (3-in) lengths and cut these lengthwise into thin slivers. Heat the oil with the butter or margarine and toss the leeks in it for 5–6 minutes, until softened. Add the mushrooms and continue to stir-fry. When they are cooked through but still slightly crisp, season with soy sauce, toss thoroughly and serve as soon as possible.

500 g (1 lb) leeks, trimmed

3 tbls sesame oil

25 g (1 oz) butter or margarine

175 g (6 oz) mushrooms, quartered

a little soy sauce

# Rice with Black Beans and Ginger

SERVES 6

Wonderfully warming, comforting food for a winter's day, this is among my very favourite recipes. The zest of ginger, the touch of garlic, are perfect highlights for this combination of rice and black beans. The cheese enriches this dish, which can also be served as a meal in its own right.

Drain the black beans and simmer in fresh water to cover with the dried herbs until tender, about 20 minutes. Drain and mix with the cooked rice. Toss in the garlic, cheese and ginger and stir over a low heat until the cheese has melted. Put into a warm serving dish.

175 g (6oz) black beans, soaked overnight

2 tbls dried mixed herbs

175 g (6 oz) rice, cooked

2 large cloves of garlic

50 g (2 oz) Cheddar cheese, grated

5-cm (2-in) piece of root ginger, finely grated

# Comforting Puddings

*Around the house flakes fly faster,*
*And all the berries are now gone*
*From holly and cotonea-aster*
*Around the house. The flakes fly! — faster*
*Shutting indoors that crumb-outcaster*
*We used to see upon the lawn*
*Around the house. Flakes fly faster*
*And all the berries now are gone.*

Thomas Hardy, *Birds at Winter Nightfall*

## Chestnut and Chocolate Gâteau

SERVES 6

You won't believe this until you try it. Light, moist and delicate, it is a perfect pudding course for a weekend lunch in winter – followed, of course, by that long brisk walk in the frosty outdoors!

Line two 20-cm (8-in) sandwich tins with Bakewell paper. Melt the chocolate with 4 tbls of water. Beat the egg yolks with the sugar until thick. Add the melted chocolate to the chestnut purée and mash until smooth (or liquidize it in the food processor). Beat into the egg yolk mixture. Whisk the egg whites until stiff and fold in. Bake at gas mark 4/180°C/350°F for 40–45 minutes. Cool on a rack. When cold, turn out and sandwich with the chocolate cream.

75 g (3 oz) plain chocolate

4 large eggs, separated

250 g (8 oz) caster sugar

250 g (8 oz) chestnut purée

150 ml ($\frac{1}{4}$ pt) chocolate cream (see p. 99)

## Carrot Pudding

SERVES 6

This excellent moist pudding makes an original and warming course; family fare, really, with a definite air of the country about it. We love this fruity cake served with freshly made *crème anglaise* (see p. 149).

Cream the margarine with the sugar and beat in the eggs. Fold in the carrots and fruit. Sift the flour with the baking powder, salt and spices and fold into the mixture. Bake in a well-greased cake tin at gas mark 4/180°C/350°F until a knife comes out clean from the centre, about 40–45 minutes. Serve warm.

125 g (4 oz) margarine

125 g (4 oz) brown sugar

2 eggs, beaten

250 g (8 oz) carrots, grated

2 tbls candied peel

125 g (4 oz) raisins

250 g (8 oz) currants

175 g (6 oz) plain flour

1 tsp baking powder

$\frac{1}{2}$ tsp salt

1 tsp ground nutmeg

1 tsp ground cinnamon

## Pineapple Upside-down Cake

SERVES 6

My children's winter favourite. This cake is gooey yet light, easy to make, and disappears at a sitting. A brilliant dessert.

Drain the pineapple and crush it. Melt 50 g (2 oz) of butter and pour into a 20-cm (8-in) square baking tin. Sprinkle on the brown sugar and then put the pineapple and nuts on top.

Cream the rest of the butter with the caster sugar and add the beaten eggs. Sift the flour with the baking powder and a pinch of salt and add gradually, with the milk, to the butter mixture. Beat thoroughly.

Pour the cake batter into the tin and cook at gas mark 4/180°C/350°F for 25–30 minutes. Cool a little, then cut into squares and serve warm, with custard.

400-g (14-oz) can of pineapple

150 g (5 oz) butter

50 g (2 oz) soft, light-brown sugar

50 g (2 oz) mixed nuts, chopped

125 g (4 oz) caster sugar

2 eggs, beaten

250 g (8 oz) plain flour

2 tsp baking powder

pinch of salt

300 ml ($\frac{1}{2}$ pt) milk

## Almond Apples

SERVES 6

This is yet another recipe given to me by a friend. I think in the winter we must talk more about food, perhaps to comfort ourselves about the appalling weather that we suffer! Anyway, talking we were, and I was lucky enough to come away with this wonderful recipe.

Peel, core and slice the apples and toss them in a little sugar. Put them into a large ovenproof dish and add a little water.

Place all the other ingredients into the blender and whizz them until well blended. Spread this crumbly mixture over the apples and cook at gas mark 4/180°C/350°F for 45 minutes. Serve hot or cold, with cream.

500 g (1 lb) apples (Bramleys, if possible)

sugar to taste

125 g (4 oz) ground almonds

125 g (4 oz) butter

125 g (4 oz) caster sugar

a few drops of almond essence

1 egg yolk

*Spring*

# Spring

# Spring

## New Shoots

*Spring goeth all in white,*
*Crowned with milk-white may:*
*In fleecy flocks of light*
*O'er heaven the white clouds stray:*

*White butterflies in the air;*
*White daisies prank the ground:*
*The cherry and hoary pear*
*Scatter their snow around.*

Robert Bridges

## Nettle Soup with Croûtons

SERVES 4

Nettles are perhaps the best known of the wild plants that can be used in cooking. Most people have heard of nettle soup for the good reason that it is simply delicious. In the old days, as soon as the young shoots pushed their way through the ground after the lean, bleak days of winter, the housewife would gather them as welcome greens to vary the boring diet of salted meat that had prevailed during the previous months. Nettles were known to be nutritious, too: they have a high vitamin C content and are a good source of minerals. One of the delights of early spring is to go out gathering young nettles (with your rubber gloves on!) to make this soup, with its bright, rich-green colour and sublime flavour.

Gather the young tops of nettles in early spring, or as they reappear after cutting back later in the year. Wearing rubber gloves, nip off the top 4–6 leaves from the stem. Wash them thoroughly when you get home, and put them into a large saucepan. Cook them as you would spinach, in their own water, with a little salt if you like, and stir from time to time. They will cook right down, and after about 10 minutes should be well softened. (The sting disappears in the boiling!) Drain thoroughly.

Melt the margarine in a heavy pan, add the flour and stir until well blended. Pour in the stock gradually, stirring as the mixture thickens. Simmer for 5 minutes and season to taste. Mix in the cooked nettles and liquidize the soup. Thin out with single cream, check the seasoning, and serve piping hot, with croûtons.

1 large saucepan full of young nettle tops

40 g (1½ oz) sunflower margarine

25 g (1 oz) plain flour

900 ml (1½ pts) stock (see p. 149)

salt and pepper

a little single cream

croûtons

119

## Spicy Baby Carrot and Orange Soup

SERVES 4

The tender taste of baby carrots when they first appear on the market in late spring always surprises me with its delicacy. A friend of mine gave me this soup as part of a fabulous Sunday lunch one May, and I was smitten with how the subtle flavour of the young carrots was enhanced, rather than overwhelmed, by gentle spicing and the sweet freshness of orange. The colour is stunning – mellow gold with a touch of red – and the texture smooth and thin. Wonderful.

Melt the margarine and sweat the onions and carrots in it for 20 minutes over a very gentle heat, stirring frequently and taking care that the vegetables do not brown. Add the curry paste and stir for 1–2 minutes before gradually adding the stock. Bring to the boil and simmer gently for a further 20 minutes. Liquidize. Add the orange juice and the cream, heat through, check the seasoning and it is ready to serve. Excellent with fresh granary rolls or with garlic bread.

40 g (1½ oz) sunflower margarine

125 g (4 oz) onion, chopped

500 g (1 lb) baby carrots, thinly sliced

1 tbls curry paste

600 ml (1 pt) stock (see p. 149)

300 ml (½ pt) freshly squeezed orange juice

150 ml (¼ pt) single cream

salt to taste

*A pleasant and happy life does not come from external things; man draws from within himself, as from a spring, pleasure and joy.*

Plutarch

## Morel Mousse

SERVES 4–6

Mushroom hunting in late spring is one of the great delights of living in the country. Armed with a large flat basket and wellington boots, I have often set off with my children, on what they rightly regard as a treasure hunt, to the beech woods to forage for fungi. The morel is a rare find, but incomparable if you have either the luck or the patience to discover where it grows (and it's usually in a different spot each year!). Failing this magical expedition, use the unusual mushrooms now to be found on the supermarket shelf: shiitake, chestnut or oyster.

Slice one quarter of the mushrooms into quarters, then each quarter into 5 thin slices. Decorate the base of a lightly greased 20-cm (8-in) soufflé dish by laying them around in circles.

Chop the rest of the mushrooms finely and cook gently in the butter for 8–10 minutes. When well cooked down, add two thirds of them to the *sauce à la crème* and purée it in the blender. Add the wine and mix well. Season to taste with salt and pepper, and chill over ice cubes in the refrigerator for 30 minutes.

Beat in the chilled cream gradually, then fold in the stiffly beaten egg whites. Pour half of the mixture carefully over the circles of sliced mushrooms in the soufflé dish, then make a layer with the remaining third of chopped mushrooms. Cover with the rest of the main mixture and place in a tray of hot water. Bake in a pre-heated oven at gas mark 4/180°C/350°F for 30 minutes. Leave to stand for 5 minutes before turning out. Delicious hot, warm or cold.

750 g (1½ lb) morels

40 g (1½ oz) butter or sunflower margarine

150 ml (¼ pt) *sauce à la crème* (see p. 148)

2 tbls white wine

salt and pepper

150 ml (¼ pt) double cream, chilled

2 egg whites, stiffly beaten

121

## Feuilletés with Spring Vegetables

SERVES 4

These golden pastry parcels, filled with finely sliced, steamed vegetables and chopped spring herbs, never fail to be popular. The smell as the herbs are cooking is a sure sign that winter is over and the growing season has begun! The *sauce printanière* that I like to serve with them always reminds me of spring, too; not just because of its name, but because of its pale, bright green colour. These *feuilletés* make a delicious lunch or supper dish, served simply with a leafy side salad.

Slice the vegetables elegantly into slim diagonal strips and cook in the unsalted butter until well coated, about 1–2 minutes. Mix in the chopped herbs and sorrel, toss in the pan for a further minute or two, and season with a little salt and pepper. Cool.

Roll the pastry out thinly and cut into 8 squares of 12.5 cm (5 in). Pile one eighth of the vegetable mixture on to the centre of each square, and fold up the corners over to the top centre. Moisten the corners with water and pinch them together hard so that they hold together. Brush with beaten egg and bake in a pre-heated oven at gas mark 6/200°C/400°F until puffed and golden brown, about 15 minutes. Serve as soon as possible, with *sauce printanière*.

*To make the* sauce printanière: Slice the vegetables finely and soften them in the butter for about 10 minutes over a gentle heat. Mix into the *sauce à la crème* and purée in the food processor to a smooth, green sauce. Season to taste with salt and pepper, thin out as necessary with single cream or milk, and heat through.

750 g (1½ lb) selection of broccoli, baby carrots, mushrooms, baby leeks, petits pois, all steamed lightly so that they are still crisp

40 g (1½ oz) unsalted butter

1 small bunch of spring herbs such as thyme, golden marjoram, chives, tansy and lovage, finely chopped

a few sorrel leaves, shredded

salt and pepper

400 g (14 oz) puff pastry

1 egg, beaten

*For the* sauce printanière

75 g (3 oz) of a green vegetable such as French beans, peas, mange-tout, asparagus, etc., lightly steamed

75 g (3 oz) butter

300 ml (½ pt) *sauce à la crème* (see p. 148)

salt and pepper

3–4 tbls single cream or milk

## Lunchtime in Springtime

The country habit has me by the heart.
He is bewitched forever who has seen,
Not with his eyes but with his vision, Spring
Flow down the woods and stipple leaves with sun,
As each man knows the life that fits him best,
The shape it makes in his soul, the tune, the tone,
And after ranging on a tentative flight . . .

V. Sackville-West, *The Land*

## Cold Leeks with Olives

SERVES 4

Young leeks, to my mind, are among the finest of our late-winter and early-spring vegetables – white and tender, with a delicate flavour that is almost better cold than hot. This combination, with good-quality black olives and the first chives and parsley of spring, is wonderful as an hors-d'œuvre.

Cut the baby leeks into thin diagonal slices. Steam until very tender, about 20 minutes or so. Cool a little, then mix with the olives and sprinkle with sea salt. Put into a shallow serving dish and sprinkle the herbs over the top. Trickle the oil over them, then finally sprinkle with the chopped walnuts. Serve at room temperature.

500 g (1 lb) small leeks, washed and trimmed

125 g (4 oz) good-quality black olives, stoned and halved

sea salt

2 tbls chives, chopped

1 tbls parsley, chopped

5 tbls walnut oil

2 tbls walnuts, chopped

## Prawns in Sesame Sauce

SERVES 4

This spicy sauce has a tang very reminiscent of Mexican cooking, which was the inspiration for this recipe.

Stir-fry the sesame seeds, pumpkin seeds and garlic in the vegetable oil over a medium heat for 3 minutes or so. Add the curry powder and lemon juice and stir together well. Gradually add the stock and heat through, stirring, for another 3 minutes. Liquidize the sauce to a smooth purée.

Brush the peeled prawns with olive oil and sprinkle with the dried herbs. Grill lightly on both sides, then put into 4 warmed ramekin dishes. Spoon a little of the sauce over each one, garnish the top with a coriander leaf and serve immediately.

3 tbls sesame seeds

2 tbls pumpkin seeds

1 clove of garlic, crushed

3 tbls vegetable oil

1 tsp curry powder

2 tsp lemon juice

150 ml ($\frac{1}{4}$ pt) stock (see p. 149)

500 g (1 lb) prawns, peeled

olive oil

1 tbls dried mixed herbs

*Garnish*

coriander leaves

## Linguini with Chicory and Spring Herbs

SERVES 4

Chicory is at its crispest and best in the spring, and it is always a welcome sight on the supermarket shelf after its winter absence. I love it in salads, yet have always secretly thought that it is even better cooked than raw. It changes completely, the flavour becoming delicate and subtle, the texture mouth-wateringly soft. In this stunning pasta dish, it is shredded and creamed with spring herbs, garlic and pimento.

Steam the chicory until very tender, about 8–10 minutes. Melt the butter or margarine and soften the garlic and herbs in it for 3–4 minutes. Stir in the chicory and pimento. Stir thoroughly over a gentle heat, and mix in the cream. Season to taste.

As you are preparing the vegetables, cook the linguini in boiling water until *al dente*, about 6–8 minutes. Drain well and toss with the chicory mixture. Serve immediately on warmed plates, with a pepper mill and grated Parmesan to hand around.

2 large heads of chicory, shredded

50 g (2 oz) butter or sunflower margarine

1 large clove of garlic, crushed

2 tbls spring herbs, chopped, such as lovage, chives, parsley, tansy, etc.

1 canned pimento, cut into short, thin slices

5 tbls single cream

350 g (12 oz) linguini

salt and pepper

*Garnish*

Parmesan cheese, grated

## Mussels with Fennel

SERVES 4

The delicate and inimitable flavour of mussels is set off to perfection by this light sauce of herbs and vegetables. A dash of cream, a little wine, and you have a memorable hors-d'œuvre.

Put the mussels into a large pan with the shallot, parsley, thyme and wine. Open them over a gentle heat, shaking the pan from time to time. Reserving the liquid, take the mussels out and remove them from their shells. Keep them warm in an ovenproof dish, covered so that they do not dry out. Strain the stock through fine muslin into another saucepan and add the julienned vegetables and the chopped fennel. Simmer together for about 5 minutes, until the vegetables are tender but still slightly crisp. Add the cream and heat through. Season to taste. Spoon the sauce over the mussels and sprinkle with the chopped fennel leaves. Serve as soon as possible.

2 kg (4½ lb) mussels, washed and the beards removed

1 shallot, finely chopped

sprig of parsley

sprig of thyme

5 tbls white wine

50 g (2 oz) carrots, cut into julienne strips

50 g (2 oz) leeks, cut into julienne strips

175 g (6 oz) Florence fennel, finely chopped

a little single cream

salt and pepper

*Garnish*

fennel leaves, chopped

# Spring Terrine

SERVES 6

This lovely loaf, with its gentle colours and soft texture, is one of my stand-bys for a special lunch. I use the first herbs of spring to flavour the vegetables – a different one for each – so that each layer of the terrine is quite distinctive. Serve it sliced, with buttered potatoes and a side salad, and pass around a bowl of *sauce printanière* (see p. 122) to make it feel even more like spring.

Soften the mushrooms in the butter or margarine and add the parsley. Cook for a further 5 minutes until well reduced. Drain off any juices and purée the mixture in the food processor with 2 tbls of the single cream. Likewise, purée the cauliflower with the chives and 2 tbls of the cream, and the carrots with the lovage and the remaining cream. Season each mixture to taste. Mix one beaten egg into each one of the mixtures.

Grease a 1-kg (2-lb) loaf tin and put the mushroom mixture into the bottom. Cover with the cauliflower mixture and then with the carrot mixture. Stand the tin in a larger tin of hot water and bake in the pre-heated oven at gas mark 6/200°C/400°F until set in the centre, about 1 hour. A sharp knife plunged into the middle will come out clean when it is done. Cool for at least 10 minutes before attempting to turn it out, and then cut into slices. Serve warm or cold, with the *sauce printanière* on p. 122.

250 g (8 oz) mushrooms, sliced

40 g (1½ oz) butter or sunflower margarine

2 tbls parsley, chopped

6 tbls single cream

1 medium cauliflower, steamed

2 tbls chives, chopped

250 g (8 oz) young carrots, steamed

2 tbls lovage, chopped

3 eggs, each beaten separately

salt and pepper

# Melting Mille-feuilles

**SERVES 8**

These light, golden pastry triangles are filled with grated courgettes and mange-tout mixed with gooey Gruyère. They are mouth-wateringly irresistible, with the flavours of coriander and asparagus in the sauce enhancing the delicate tastes of the vegetables. This is a main course for special occasions and no one who has had it will easily forget the experience!

Roll the pastry out fairly thinly and cut into 16 rectangles measuring about 5 × 13 cm (2 × 5 in). Brush each one with beaten egg and place on a well-greased baking tray. Cook in a pre-heated oven at gas mark 6/200°C/400°F until risen and golden, about 8–10 minutes. Split the pastry puffs lengthwise one third of the way up their height, and keep in a warm oven.

Next liquidize the peas and asparagus with the *sauce à la crème* until smooth. Thin out with cream and heat through gently. Set aside.

Toss the courgettes and mange-tout in the butter until well coated, then mix in the coriander and the cheese. Season to taste with sea salt and pepper. Toss the mixture in the prepared sauce so that it is lightly coated and heat through until piping hot (a microwave is ideal for this). Pile on to the bottom layer of the warm pastry rectangles, cover with the top layer, and they are ready to serve.

875 g (1¾ lb) puff pastry

1 egg, beaten

*For the sauce*

175 g (6 oz) peas, cooked

175 g (6 oz) asparagus, cooked

150 ml (¼ pt) *sauce à la crème* (see p. 148)

3–4 tbls single cream

*For the filling*

750 g (1½ lb) courgettes, coarsely grated

350 g (12 oz) mange-tout, diagonally sliced

75 g (3 oz) unsalted butter

1 medium bunch of coriander, finely chopped

175 g (6 oz) Gruyère cheese, cut into tiny cubes

sea salt and pepper

## Traditional Spring Festivals

'Tis time, I think, by Wenlock town
The golden broom should blow;
The hawthorn sprinkled up and down
Should charge the land with snow.

Spring will not wait the loiterer's time
Who keeps so long away;
So others wear the broom and climb
The hedgerows heaped with may.

Oh tarnish late on Wenlock edge,
Gold that I never see;
Lie long, high snowdrifts in the hedge
That will not shower on me.

A. E. Housman, *A Shropshire Lad*

## Simnel Cake

### MAKES A 1 KG (2½ LB) CAKE

A Simnel cake is a Mothering Sunday cake, traditionally part of a mid-Lent feast when all the children and godchildren of the family got together and received the blessing of their mother, after presenting her with a trinket or a posy of spring flowers. These cakes varied from region to region and were still being made in the 1950s, although the custom seems to have largely died out today. A pity, for this particular one is a glorious English cake, and it keeps well. The traditional decoration of 11 paste balls on the top represents the 11 faithful Apostles – a pointed absence of Judas – and a large one in the centre represents Christ himself.

Sift the flour with the salt, baking powder and spices. Cream the butter with the lemon rind, juice and sugar until pale and creamy. Beat in the egg yolks and fold in one third of the flour mixture. Beat thoroughly. Whisk the egg whites until they are very stiff and fold them in alternately with the remaining flour and all the fruits. Put one half of the mixture into a well-greased 20-cm (8-in) cake tin. Cover with one third of the almond paste (see below), rolled out and cut to fit the circumference of the tin. Cover with the remaining cake mixture. Bake at gas mark 3/170°C/325°F until set and firm, about 2 hours.

Allow the cake to cool for 15 minutes. Brush with the warmed jam. Roll out the remaining almond paste and cut it into a circle to crown the cake. Make a crisscross diamond pattern, using the back of a knife. Make 11 balls from the paste trimmings and put them around the edge and a large ball for the centre. Brush the cake with beaten egg and sprinkle with caster

250 g (8 oz) plain flour

pinch of salt

½ tsp baking powder

½ tsp mixed spice

½ tsp ground cinnamon

½ tsp ground cloves

150 g (5 oz) butter

grated rind and juice of 1 lemon

125 g (4 oz) sugar

3 eggs, separated

125 g (4 oz) sultanas

250 g (8 oz) currants

125 g (4 oz) glacé cherries

25 g (1 oz) candied peel

2 tsp apricot jam, warmed

1 small egg, beaten

caster sugar

*For the almond paste*

350 g (12 oz) ground almonds

350 g (12 oz) icing sugar, sifted

3 large egg yolks

2 tsp lemon juice

1 tsp almond essence

1 tsp vanilla essence

1 tbls brandy

sugar. Put under a gentle grill until it turns golden. Decorate with more glacé fruits, and tie it around the side with a wide ribbon.

This Simnel cake will keep well in an air-tight tin, well wrapped, for a week or two.

*To make the almond paste:* Mix the ground almonds with the icing sugar. Beat the egg yolks with the lemon juice, almond essence, vanilla and brandy, and mix into the ground almond mixture. Knead until it is smooth. Chill.

## St David's Day Leek Tart

SERVES 4

Nobody really knows why St David, the sixth-century abbot-bishop who is remembered in so many place-names in west Wales, is so closely associated with leeks, but the connection was as established in Shakespeare's time as it is today. The leek is much in evidence on 1 March, his saint's day, so, having high regard for Wales and Welshness, I make this leek dish every year in honour of their national saint, and very good it is, too.

Slice the leeks thinly and soften them in the olive oil and butter mixed, over a gentle heat, until very soft. Beat 2 of the eggs with the cream and half of the cheese, mix with the leeks and liquidize to a rough purée. Season to taste with salt, pepper and mace, and put the mixture into the pastry shell. Make 4 little 'nests' and break the remaining eggs into them. Cover with the rest of the grated cheese, grind some black pepper over the top and bake at gas mark 5/190°C/375°F until the eggs are lightly set, about 20–25 minutes. Serve immediately.

750 g (1½ lb) leeks, sliced

3–4 tbls olive oil

25 g (1 oz) butter

6 eggs

100 ml (4 fl oz) double cream

75 g (3 oz) hard cheese, grated

salt and pepper

1–2 tsp ground of mace

22-cm (9-in) shortcrust pastry case, baked blind

freshly ground black pepper

# Shrovetide Soufflé Pancakes

SERVES 6

Pancake Day, or Shrove Tuesday, has more customs associated with it than any other festival apart from Christmas. On the days before Lent began, it was traditional to feast before the fast, to have a great blow-out and clear the larder – in some places these days were called 'Bursting Saturday' or 'Guttit Day'! Pancake races are still held in various parts of the country, local football teams gather for a game, and church bells ring to summon the people to church to be 'shriven', cleansed of their sins before Lent begins. Here is a modern way to celebrate a well-established festival: soufflés wrapped up inside light pancakes, elegant and delicious food.

Put all the pancake ingredients and 150 ml (¼ pt) water into the food processor and blend until smooth. Leave to stand in a cool place for 3 hours. Make in the usual way.

Melt the margarine and stir in the flour until smooth. Gradually add the warmed milk, stirring all the time, until the sauce is thick and smooth. Cook over a very low heat for 5 minutes. Add the cheeses and stir until they melt. Add the chives and season to taste with salt, pepper and cayenne. Remove from the heat and cool a little.

Beat the egg yolks thoroughly and stir them into the cheese mixture. Whisk the whites until they are very stiff and fold them in. Heap the soufflé filling on to each pancake equally, fold the pancake over the top and place carefully in a large ovenproof dish. Sprinkle with the Parmesan and bake at gas mark 6/200°C/400°F until well risen, about 10 minutes. Serve immediately.

*For the pancakes*

150 g (5 oz) plain flour

2 large eggs

300 ml (½ pt) milk

½ tsp salt

*For the soufflé filling*

25 g (1 oz) sunflower margarine

2 tbls plain flour

150 ml (¼ pt) milk, warmed

40 g (1½ oz) Gruyère cheese, grated

40 g (1½ oz) Cheddar cheese, grated

2 tbls Parmesan cheese, grated

2 tbls chives, chopped

salt and pepper

cayenne

3 eggs, separated

## St Valentine's Pastries

MAKES 12

A favourite East Anglian caper for children was to go around singing for alms before sunrise on St Valentine's Day, and traditionally they would be given coins, or fruit, or these special pastry cakes filled with chopped preserved plums. St Valentine's Day has been popular for many generations: the patron saint of lovers is commemorated by the exchange of gifts, often secretly and anonymously. There is a quaint ancient belief that birds choose their mates on St Valentine's Day.

Press the sweet crust pastry dough into 12 well-greased individual bun tins.

Cream the sugar into the butter or margarine until pale and smooth. Beat in the eggs and, when thoroughly mixed, stir in the almond essence and the ground almonds mixed with the baking powder.

Spread the bottom of each pastry shell with some plum jam. Fill it up with the almond mixture and sprinkle the top with flaked almonds. Bake at gas mark 3/170°C/325°F until risen and golden, about 25–30 minutes. Cool on a rack and lift out when still warm. Serve cold and as fresh as possible.

500 g (1 lb) sweet crust pastry dough (see p. 149)

75 g (3 oz) sugar

75 g (3 oz) butter or margarine

2 eggs, beaten

2 tsp almond essence

50 g (2 oz) ground almonds

$\frac{1}{2}$ tsp baking powder

3 tbls almonds, flaked

4–5 tbls plum jam (preferably home-made)

# Maundy Gingerbread Buttons

MAKES 12

There is a Maundy Thursday fair held at Tombland in Norwich where these 'button' biscuits are sold. Brown ones, like the ones here, are flavoured with spice and chopped peel, and there are white ones, too, that are flavoured with lemon. It seems that whatever the festive season, serious or joyful, the English will establish a traditional recipe for it! This is one such local example: a token for the day before Good Friday to make for your loved ones. 'Maund' is an old word for a gift.

Melt the margarine, sugar and honey over a gentle heat, stirring until the sugar dissolves. Sift the flour with the ginger and soda bicarbonate, and make a well in the centre. Pour in the melted mixture and mix well. Add enough egg to form a soft dough, then allow to cool slightly.

Roll the dough out thinly and cut into gingerbread-men shapes with a cutter. Place on lightly greased baking trays and press a little peel into the centre of each one. Bake at gas mark 5/190°C/375°F for 8–10 minutes, then remove carefully and cool on a rack.

50 g (2 oz) sunflower margarine

75 g (3 oz) light-brown sugar

2 tbls runny honey

200 g (7 oz) plain flour

3 tsp ground ginger

1 tsp soda bicarbonate

1 egg, beaten

25 g (1 oz) mixed peel, chopped

*When thou hast enough, remember the time of hunger.*

Ecclesiastes

## An Easter Feast

Nothing is so beautiful as spring —
   When weeds, in wheels, shoot long and lovely and lush;
   Thrush's eggs look like little low heavens, and thrush
Through the echoing timber does so rinse and wring
The ear, it strikes like lightnings to hear him sing;
   The glassy peartree leaves and blooms, they brush
   The descending blue; that blue is all in a rush
With richness; the racing lambs too have fair their fling.

What is all this juice and all this joy?
   A strain of the earth's sweet being in the beginning
In Eden garden. — Have, get, before it cloy,
   Before it cloud. Christ, lord, and sour with sinning,
Innocent mind and Mayday in girl and boy,
   Most, O maid's child, thy choice and worthy the winning.

Gerard Manley Hopkins, *Spring*

## Greek Olive Pâté

SERVES 8

I love Easter. For me it is a very special festival, with its symbolism of regeneration and hope. So I make a fuss of Easter Sunday, filling the house with spring flowers and preparing a wonderful feast. The Greeks always celebrate with lavish food and traditional festivities, so in honour of a country that I love I have invented this recipe to get the feast off to a good start.

Purée the cottage cheese in the food processor, and then add the feta and oil and purée again. Chop the olives very finely and mix them in with the crushed garlic, pepper and thyme. Chill, and serve with warm pitta bread cut into strips.

250 g (8 oz) cottage cheese

250 g (8 oz) feta cheese

2–3 tbls Greek olive oil

18–20 black olives, pitted

garlic to taste

freshly ground pepper

2 tbls thyme, chopped

## Seafood Spectacular

SERVES 8

Spectacular this recipe is indeed. It takes quite a lot of preparation, but for some wonderful dishes there are no short cuts.

Cook the spinach in its own water until tender, then drain thoroughly and chop finely. Cool it, then squeeze it completely dry. Mix into the béchamel and season. Chill.

Prepare all the seafood: open the mussels over a gentle heat, and reserve the liquid, straining it through fine muslin. Peel the prawns, remove the crab meat from its shell, and steam the white fish until lightly cooked, about 5 minutes. Skin it and remove the bones.

Make a stock from the prawn and crab shells: cover with water, add the bay leaf and dried mixed herbs, and simmer for 15 minutes, covered. Cool, then strain off. Melt the butter and stir in the flour, then gradually add 450 ml ($\frac{3}{4}$ pt) of the warm stock, stirring until the sauce thickens and becomes smooth. Simmer for 5 minutes over a very low heat, then stir in the cream. Flavour with the tarragon and season to taste. Stir in the prepared seafood. Chill.

Assemble in a large ovenproof dish, about 20 cm × 20 cm (8 in × 8 in) square and 10 cm (4 in) deep. Put alternating strips of the spinach and seafood mixtures cross-wise in the dish. Cut two thirds of the filo sheets to fit the shape of the serving dish. Brush each one with oil and place on top of the seafood and spinach mixture. Cut the remaining sheets into a fish shape, brush each one with oil and place on top. Bake at gas mark 5/190°C/375°F until the pastry is well risen, golden and crisp, about 20–25 minutes. Serve piping hot.

1 kg (2 lb) spinach leaf, washed

300 ml ($\frac{1}{2}$ pt) thick béchamel sauce (see p. 148)

1.25 kg ($2\frac{1}{2}$ lb) mixed seafood, such as mussels, prawns, crab, cockles, scallops and white fish

1 bay leaf

1 tbls dried mixed herbs

40 g ($1\frac{1}{2}$ oz) butter

3 tbls plain flour

150 ml ($\frac{1}{4}$ pt) single cream

3 tbls tarragon, chopped

salt and pepper

18 sheets of filo pastry, each measuring 15 cm (6 in) square

olive oil

## Fresh Noodles with Mushrooms

SERVES 8

This side dish of fresh pasta and wild mushrooms, coated in a light cream sauce flavoured with dill, is mouth-watering. It is in perfect balance with the seafood, and turns the main course into a feast indeed.

Slice the mushrooms and sauté them gently in the butter. When they are soft, stir in the dill and add the cream. Heat through and fold this mixture into the drained, hot noodles. Serve as soon as possible.

350 g (12 oz) mushrooms such as shiitake, chestnut or wild

75 g (3 oz) unsalted butter

3 tbls dill, chopped

150 ml (¼ pt) single cream

350 g (12 oz) fresh noodles, cooked *al dente*

## Baby Carrots with Sesame Seeds

SERVES 8

Easter is the time when the very first baby carrots come on to the market, and I cannot resist including them in my Easter feast. Succulent and full of flavour, they are a real treat. Here, stir-fried in sesame oil and served with toasted sesame seeds sprinkled on top, they are at their best.

Stir-fry the carrots in the oil over a moderate heat until they begin to soften, then turn the heat down, cover the pan and cook until they are *al dente*, about 3–4 minutes. Put in a warm serving dish and toss with the toasted sesame seeds just before serving.

1 kg (2 lb) baby carrots, cut lengthwise

5 tbls sesame oil

6 tbls sesame seeds, toasted

138

## Easter Salad

SERVES 8

This is one of my favourite salads: a tempting mixture of fruits and leaves, all dressed in a blue-cheese vinaigrette. I serve it as a separate course, and at a leisurely pace, so that there is time to work up an appetite for the wonderful dessert that is to follow.

Toss all the salad ingredients together and dress with the blue-cheese vinaigrette (see below).

*To make the blue-cheese vinaigrette:* Stir the cheese into the vinaigrette and blend them together thoroughly – you can do this in the liquidizer for a really smooth and creamy dressing.

flesh of 1 large ripe avocado, diced

2 pears, cored, peeled and thinly sliced

1 large yellow pepper, de-seeded and chopped

2 crisp lettuces, washed and torn into small pieces

*For the blue-cheese vinaigrette*

50 g (2 oz) blue cheese, mashed

150 ml ($\frac{1}{4}$ pt) vinaigrette

garlic to taste, crushed (optional)

## Paskha

SERVES 8

I started this feast with something Greek and I end it with a traditional Russian Easter dessert. Historically, this is made in a pyramid-shaped mould and decorated with fresh or frozen berries and pistachio nuts.

Purée the cream cheese in the food processor with the sour cream. Cream the butter with the vanilla sugar and then beat into the cream-cheese mixture until smooth. Fold in the lemon rind, almonds, raisins, chopped cherries and vanilla. Put into a lightly greased bowl. Press down with a weighted plate and chill for 2 hours. Put into the freezer for at least 3 hours. To turn out, dip the bowl into another bowl of very hot water, and run a sharp knife around the edge to loosen. Turn out on to a plate, decorate as desired, and serve very cold, cut in wedges.

750 g (1$\frac{1}{2}$ lb) cream cheese

5–6 tbls sour cream

50 g (2 oz) unsalted butter

125 g (4 oz) vanilla sugar

grated rind of 2 lemons

40 g (1$\frac{1}{2}$ oz) almonds, blanched and chopped

125 g (4 oz) seedless raisins

75 g (3 oz) glacé cherries, chopped

2 tsp vanilla essence

139

# Spring

## Seasonal Side Vegetables

*Out of the wood of thoughts that grow by night*
*To be cut down by the sharp axe of light,*
*Out of the night, two cocks together crow,*
*Clearing the darkness with a silver blow.*
*And bright before my eyes twin trumpeters stand*
*Heralds of splendour, one at either hand,*
*Each facing each as in a coat of arms:*
*The milkers lace their boots up at the farms.*

Edward Thomas, *Cock Crow*

## Spicy Aubergines

SERVES 4

A rich, strong dish of aubergines with a touch of chilli makes a delicious side vegetable to go with a light main course. The flavours of ginger, garlic and spring onion give it an oriental quality that reveals its Japanese origins.

Sprinkle the aubergines with salt and leave them to sweat for half an hour. Pat them dry on kitchen paper and sauté in the oil, stirring frequently, for about 5 minutes. Remove with a slotted spoon and keep warm. Add the ginger, garlic and spring onions to the oil and soften them for 1–2 minutes, then stir in the chilli sauce and stock. Mix well. Return the aubergines to the pan, bring to the boil, and then put immediately into a warmed serving dish. Serve sprinkled with chopped chives.

500 g (1 lb) aubergines, cut into 2-cm ($\frac{3}{4}$-in) cubes

salt

4 tbls sesame oil

25 g (1 oz) root ginger, grated

1 clove of garlic, crushed

4 spring onions, sliced

a little chilli sauce

100 ml (4 fl oz) stock (see p. 149)

*Garnish*

chives, chopped

## Stir-fry Leeks with Mushrooms

SERVES 4

Stir-frying leeks in sesame oil gives them an indefinable quality – suffice it to say that this way of cooking them is a transformation. Coupled with lightly cooked mushrooms, this is a vegetable dish with a difference.

Slice the leeks thinly and diagonally, and stir-fry in the sesame oil until they begin to soften, about 8–10 minutes. Add the sliced mushrooms and stir-fry again, until they, too, soften and both vegetables are cooked through. Add the soy sauce, mix it in well, heat through and serve as soon as possible.

625 g (1$\frac{1}{4}$ lb) leeks, trimmed and washed

4–5 tbls sesame oil

250 g (8 oz) mushrooms, sliced

2 tbls soy sauce

## Chicory au Gratin with Rosemary

SERVES 4

Braised chicory, cooked with sprigs of rosemary so that the herb's flavour permeates the vegetable, makes a delicious and delicate gratin. I like to serve this with the Morel Mousse on p. 121.

Put the chicory into an ovenproof dish with the rosemary and a little water, and sprinkle with salt and pepper. Cover tightly with foil and bake in a pre-heated oven at gas mark 4/180°C/350°F until soft, about 30 minutes. Remove, reserving the juices, and slice into 1-cm (½-in) slices. Mix into the béchamel with the cooking liquid and season to taste. Chop a few of the rosemary leaves finely and stir them in. Put into an ovenproof serving dish and sprinkle with the breadcrumbs and cheese mixed together. Return to the oven and bake for about 10 minutes, until it is golden and crisp on top.

4 medium heads of chicory

2 large sprigs of rosemary

salt and pepper

300 ml (½ pt) béchamel sauce (see p. 148)

2 tbls dried wholemeal breadcrumbs

2 tbls Parmesan cheese, grated

## Saffron Cauliflower Purée

SERVES 8

I am very fond of vegetable purées. This one is particularly special because of the addition of saffron, that fascinating spice made from crocus stamens, which, in its time, has commanded the same price as gold.

Mix the saffron threads with the cream and allow to stand for 15 minutes. Stir it into the béchamel and heat through gently for 3 minutes. Purée the cauliflower with the sauce and season to taste with sea salt. Put into a warmed serving dish and serve hot.

2 sachets of saffron threads

5 tbls single cream

300 ml (½ pt) béchamel sauce (see p. 148)

1 large cauliflower, steamed

sea salt

## Dolly's Mushrooms

SERVES 4

These are wonderful, and so easy to make. The full flavour of fresh mushrooms comes into its own with a lightly grilled herb mixture on top of them.

Mix the herbs with the beaten eggs and season with salt and pepper. Remove the stalks from the mushrooms and cover the gill-surface of the mushrooms with the egg mixture. Place under a medium grill until the egg is set and the mushroom underneath is soft and cooked through, about 7–8 minutes. Serve piping hot.

2 tbls mixed herbs, finely chopped

2 eggs, beaten

salt and pepper

250 g (8 oz) large flat mushrooms

## Chinese Stir-fry of Spring Vegetables

SERVES 4

I adore Chinese cooking, and have adapted many of its ideas to my Western way of working. This recipe is a delightfully crisp and flavourful mixture of lightly cooked spring vegetables seasoned with the typically oriental combination of ginger, garlic and soy sauce.

Heat the oil in a wok and cook the garlic and ginger in it gently for a few minutes. Toss in all the vegetables and stir-fry until they are heated through and beginning to soften, but do not allow them to become overcooked and soggy. Stir in the soy sauce, mix thoroughly and serve immediately.

4 tbls sesame oil

1 clove of garlic, crushed

2.5-cm (1-in) piece of root ginger, grated

1 small spring cabbage, shredded

125 g (4 oz) baby carrots, cut into thin diagonal slices

250 g (8 oz) baby leeks, cut thinly and diagonally

175 g (6 oz) mushrooms, sliced

125 g (4 oz) beansprouts

2 tbls soy sauce

# Spring

## Spring Sweets

Now fades the last long streak of snow,
Now burgeons every maze of quick
About the flowering squares, and thick
By ashen roots the violets blow.

Now rings the woodland loud and long,
The distance takes a lovelier hue,
And drown'd in yonder living blue
The lark becomes a sightless song.

How dance the lights on lawn and lea,
The flocks are whiter down the vale,
And milkier every milky sail
 On winding stream or distant sea –

Tennyson, *In Memoriam*

# Gâteau à l'Orange

SERVES 6

This gâteau has become a great favourite with my friends – and it's one of mine, too, being very simple to prepare as well as utterly scrumptious. The delicious flavours of orange and almond seem to create their own sunshine, and always remind me that summer is not far off.

Beat the egg yolks with the sugar until pale and creamy. Add the ground almonds, breadcrumbs, the grated rind and juice of the orange, and the almond essence. Fold in the stiffly beaten egg whites.

Grease a soufflé dish and dust the inside with icing sugar. Turn the mixture into it and bake, standing in a tray of hot water, for 25–30 minutes in a pre-heated oven at gas mark 4/180°C/350°F. Cool on a rack, and turn out when nearly cold. Chill. Serve sprinkled with icing sugar and decorated with whipped cream if desired.

4 eggs, separated

50 g (2 oz) caster sugar

125 g (4 oz) ground almonds

2 tbls breadcrumbs

grated rind of $\frac{1}{2}$ orange

juice of 1 orange

1–2 drops almond essence

# Crunchy Treacle Tart

SERVES 4–6

A popular favourite with family and friends alike, this is a quick and easy version of the traditional English treacle tart. As spring arrives, I wish to spend far less time in the kitchen, so the quicker and easier a dessert is to prepare, the better – and this crunchy tart is just as delicious as the classic one.

Melt the margarine with the golden syrup and pour over the crushed cornflakes in a bowl. Toss them until they are well coated and put into the pastry shell. Bake in a pre-heated oven at gas mark 4/180°C/350°F for 15 minutes. Allow to cool, then chill thoroughly before serving with whipped cream.

50 g (2 oz) margarine

2 tbls golden syrup

175 g (6 oz) cornflakes, slightly crushed

20-cm (8-in) sweet crust pastry case (see p. 149), baked blind

145

## Mocha Chiffon

SERVES 4–6

A refreshing dessert, just right for the time of year when many people's thoughts are turning to outdoor activity, and when we feel we need lighter food than during the winter. This is a dessert for all occasions – family food or dinner-party food alike.

Beat the egg yolks with the sugar until smooth and creamy. Melt the chocolate in a bowl over hot water and stir it into the egg yolk mixture. Pour 60 ml (2 fl oz) of boiling water over the agar-agar, stir well, then simmer until dissolved, about 5 minutes. Add the instant coffee, stir until it dissolves and combine it with the chocolate mixture. Beat the egg whites stiffly and fold them in carefully. Transfer to individual glasses and chill for 3–4 hours. Serve sprinkled with the toasted almonds.

3 eggs, separated

175 g (6 oz) sugar

100 g (4 oz) plain chocolate

2 tsp agar-agar

2 tsp instant coffee

50 g (2 oz) almonds, toasted and finely chopped

## Apricot Yogurt Delight

SERVES 4

A light, delectable dessert to round off a springtime meal. If you can obtain dried hunza apricots (the little round ones with their stones still in the middle), do use them, because their flavour is so deliciously subtle. The creaminess of Greek yogurt in this dessert is impossible to resist.

Soak the apricots for only 30 minutes, then stone them if necessary and chop the flesh into pea-sized shapes. Mix into the yogurt. Fold the stiffly beaten egg white into the mixture and pour it into 4 individual glass dishes. Chill. Just before serving, grate the chocolate finely and sprinkle over the top.

125 g (4 oz) dried apricots

500-g (1-lb) carton of Greek yogurt

1 egg white, stiffly beaten

25 g (1 oz) plain chocolate

## Pear and Kiwi Sponge with Lemon Balm

SERVES 6

As lemon balm begins to shoot in late spring, I love to use it in salads and puddings; it goes especially well with pears. As this dish cooks, its sweet fragrance is released into the kitchen. A proper pudding.

Cream the butter or margarine with the sugar until pale and smooth, then beat in the eggs, one by one. Stir in the sliced fruit and lemon balm, and then carefully fold in the sifted flour. Grease a 20-cm (8-in) cake tin, preferably one with a removable base, and bake in a pre-heated oven at gas mark 5/190°C/375°F until risen and lightly set, about 25–30 minutes. A sharp knife plunged into the middle will come out clean when it is ready to serve. Cool on a rack, and then turn out. Serve warm or cold, sprinkled with icing sugar, and with thick cream or custard to hand around if desired.

125 g (4 oz) butter or margarine

125 g (4 oz) sugar

2 eggs

400-g (14-oz) can of pears, drained and sliced

250 g (8 oz) kiwis, peeled, quartered and sliced

a few lemon balm leaves, shredded

125 g (4 oz) self-raising flour

*Changes arouse the understanding of men and do not allow them to become torpid.*

Hippocrates

# Basic Recipes

## Béchamel Sauce

MAKES 300 ML ($\frac{1}{2}$ PT)

Melt the butter or margarine in a heavy pan and stir in the flour with a wooden spoon. Add the warm milk slowly, stirring all the time, until the sauce thickens. Season to taste, turn the heat down and simmer over a very gentle heat for 5 minutes. Thin out with more milk if necessary.

*To make* sauce à la crème: Use single cream instead of milk, or half milk and half cream.

40 g (1$\frac{1}{2}$ oz) butter or margarine

2 tbls plain flour

300 ml ($\frac{1}{2}$ pt) milk, warmed

salt and pepper

## Mayonnaise

Break the egg into the food processor, mix in the mustard and beat thoroughly. Very slowly, a few drops at a time, pour in the oil while the machine is working, and as the mixture begins to thicken you can pour a little faster, until all the oil is used up and the mayonnaise thick and glossy. Thin out with lemon juice to taste, and season with sea salt.

1 egg

1 tbls *moutarde de Meaux*

300 ml ($\frac{1}{2}$ pt) sunflower oil

lemon juice to taste

sea salt

## Melba Toast

Cut as many slices of white bread as required as thinly as possible. Remove the crusts and cut into strips about 2.5 cm (1 in) wide. Lay them on a metal baking tray and cook in a very low oven, gas mark 2/150°C/300°F, until they have turned a light golden colour, about 30–40 minutes. Cool on a rack.

## Shortcrust Pastry

MAKES A 20-CM (8-IN) PIE SHELL

Put all the ingredients and 3 tbls of water into the blender and work until a dough is formed. Knead until smooth and chill for at least 30 minutes before using.

75 g (3 oz) soft margarine

175 g (6 oz) plain flour

large pinch of salt

## Stock

I prefer to use vegetable stock for the recipes in this book, and usually I make it with stock cubes. However, if you wish to make fresh vegetable stock, here is how.

Take whatever fresh vegetables are in season, including outer cabbage leaves and other trimmings such as leek tops; onions, carrots, Jerusalem artichokes, turnips and broad beans are also excellent and give a good flavour to vegetable stock. Put them into a large saucepan and cover with cold water. Add a little salt, some whole peppercorns, a bay leaf or two, and either fresh or dried herbs. Bring to the boil and simmer, covered, for 1 hour. Leave to stand until cool, then strain off and store in the fridge until ready for use. This stock freezes very well.

## Sweet Crust Pastry

Melt the margarine and stir in the caster sugar. Cook over a gentle heat until dissolved. Off the heat, stir in the flour and work to a smooth dough. Chill for 20–30 minutes before using.

150 g (5 oz) butter or margarine

75 g (3 oz) caster sugar

250 g (8 oz) plain flour, sifted

## Crème Anglaise

MAKES 450 ML ($\frac{3}{4}$ PT)

Beat the sugar with the egg yolks or whole egg (the latter makes a lighter custard) until thick and creamy. The mixture will turn pale yellow. Beat in the cornflour. Continue beating while you pour on the hot milk in a thin stream, until the mixture is well blended. Pour into a heavy-bottomed saucepan and cook gently over a moderate heat, stirring all the time with a wooden spoon. When the custard begins to thicken and turn creamy, allow it to come to a very gentle simmer, turn the heat down and continue stirring for 1–2 minutes. Do not let the custard boil hard, otherwise it will separate. Remove from the heat and stir in the vanilla. Leave to settle for 5–10 minutes before serving. This custard can also be served cold.

75 g (3 oz) caster sugar

2 egg yolks or 1 whole egg

1 heaped tsp cornflour

450 ml ($\frac{3}{4}$ pt) milk, hot

1 tbls vanilla essence

# Herbs through the Year

## Evergreen Herbs

Bay                Sage
Rosemary           Winter Savory
Rue

## Spring Herbs

These herbs appear at the beginning of the
growing year, but last through the summer and into the early autumn. They are
particularly good to use when young, as
their flavour is at its most delicate.

Chervil      Lovage      Tansy
Chives       Marjoram    Thyme
Fennel       Parsley
Hyssop       Sorrel

## Summer Herbs

Balm         Coriander
Basil        Dill
Bergamot     Marigold
Borage       Mint
Camomile     Summer Savory
Chervil      Tarragon

# The British Cheeseboard

*Stilton* has been called the king of English cheeses. It was first sold over two centuries ago to coach passengers who stopped at the Bell Inn at Stilton, where it is still made. Its manufacture today is limited to Leicestershire, Nottinghamshire and Derbyshire, where it is turned by hand, just as it was in the eighteenth century.

Stilton is a creamy-white cheese, turning to amber near the crust, and is characterized by blue veining. This is achieved by inserting stainless steel rods during the maturing process, which allows air to penetrate and mould to develop. The cheese has a velvety texture and a strong, slightly salty taste that becomes more pungent as the cheese matures.

*White Stilton* is simply young Stilton in which blue veining has not been allowed to develop.

*Cheddar* was first recorded in the early sixteenth century, made in the dramatically beautiful Cheddar Gorge that is now world-famous for its product. Cheddar accounts for 70 per cent of all the cheese eaten in the UK. It comes in three degrees, mild, medium and mature, and its close, waxy texture and butter-gold colour are familiar to every household. Cheddar is widely used in cooking, as well as taking pride of place on the British cheeseboard.

*Caerphilly* was first made in about 1831. A relatively new cheese that originates from the Cardiff area, it is made from the milk of shorthorn cows. It is the only surviving traditional Welsh cheese, known locally as 'miner's cheese' because the miners would take bread and Caerphilly down the shafts for their lunch. It is a white, smooth cheese, slightly crumbly with a fresh mild flavour and salty after-taste.

*Wensleydale* has been made in the Yorkshire dales for the past thousand years, invented by monks at Jervaulx Abbey in the eleventh century just after the Norman Conquest. The cheese is still made today in the dales, following the ancient tradition handed down from the monks to local farmers after the dissolution of the monasteries by Henry VIII in the sixteenth century. Wensleydale has a mild taste and flaky texture, a creamy-white colour, and a gentle, smooth after-taste. *Blue Wensleydale* also has a fine reputation, having a mellower flavour than the white; it is rich and creamy, with the distinctive tang of blue cheese.

# The British Cheeseboard

*Lancashire* comes in three main types: double curd, single curd and sage. *Double Lancashire* is a rich, creamy cheese; the single variety is crumbly and dry. The green, marbled effect of *Sage Lancashire* is created by the addition of rubbed sage leaves to the curd before pressing. The cheese has a mild flavour when young, becoming more pungent if matured more than eight weeks. Originally made centuries ago, it was the staple food of mill workers in the Lancashire cotton industry.

*Cheshire* is the oldest of all the English cheeses, dating back to Roman times, and it gets a mention in the Domesday Book of 1086. A favourite cheese at the court of Queen Elizabeth I, it originates from the Chester area, but today is also made in Shropshire, north-east Wales and the Dee valley. Cheshire is usually white, but there are also red and blue varieties. The former was originally coloured with carrot juice, but today annatto is used, a natural extract from the seed pods of a tropical tree. *Blue Cheshire* cheese is made only on local farms. Cheshire has a distinctive salty tang, which it gets from salt-springs that lie under the pastures on which the cattle are fed. It is second in popularity only to Cheddar.

*Derbyshire* is similar in texture to Cheddar, but is even moister and more delicate in flavour. It is a mild cheese when young, becoming fuller and darker in colour when mature. Not very much is produced, so it is quite an unusual addition to a cheeseboard. *Sage Derby*, originally manufactured for harvest time and Christmas, is now made all the year round. Sage is blended into the cheese to give it the distinctive flavour of the herb, and a green, marbled effect.

*Red Leicester* is the most highly coloured of all the English cheeses, a bright, russet red that traditionally came from the addition of beetroot or carrot juice to the milk. Nowadays annatto is used. Red Leicester is made throughout Leicestershire and the eastern shires. It is moister than Cheddar, and is a flaky, semi-hard cheese with a clean, fresh flavour.

*Double Gloucester* was originally made from the rich, late-season milk of Gloucestershire cattle. 'Double' Gloucester got its name because it was made from full-cream milk taken from two milkings. Like Red Leicester and Cheshire, it is coloured with annatto, and has a bright, golden-red colour and waxy texture. One of the most aristocratic of British cheeses.

*Tendale* is a newcomer to the British cheeseboard, designed to suit the modern health-conscious diet. It is a reduced-fat cheese that comes in two varieties, one Cheddar-like and one Cheshire-like. It is a hard-pressed cheese that is sold in pre-packed wedges. Tendale contains half the fat and energy content of full-fat cheese and one third more protein.

*Lymeswold* was launched on the British market in October 1982 and has established itself alongside the most distinguished of our traditional cheeses. It is the first new, natural British cheese for centuries, and is made in four varieties.

*Mild Blue Lymeswold* is a pale, cream-coloured cheese streaked with blue and encased in a white, velvety rind. It has a delicate buttery taste with the distinctive tang of a blue cheese. It is made in Aston and traditional cheese-making methods are used.

*Creamy-white Lymeswold* is a soft, mould-ripened cheese. This variety is very creamy in texture and has a delicate butter flavour. It is made with milk and fresh dairy cream, set with rennet and a special starter culture. It has a soft, white, edible rind similar to that of Brie.

*Lymeswold English Country Brie* has a tasty, mellow flavour, which is achieved by a mould-ripening process. It makes a soft cheese with a very creamy texture, made with whole milk and added rennet. A white mould culture makes the velvety outer skin. *Country Brie* develops during storage to a rounder, mellower taste as it matures.

Five soft-spreading cheeses fall under the general title of *Lymeswold Country Recipe Soft Brie*: two fruit-flavoured and three savoury. Fresh, full-cream milk is used to make smooth, creamy cheeses flavoured with pineapple; apple; onion and watercress; herbs and garlic; and spring onion and dill.

*Goat cheeses*, previously imported mainly from France, are now quite widely produced on farms and homesteads in Britain. Some are soft cheeses that are wonderful for cooking with, as well as for spreading on bread; others are medium-hard to hard, with the characteristic dry taste of classic goat cheese. A small round on the cheeseboard adds interest and variety to a selection of British cheeses.

# Conversion Tables

## Solid Measures

| Metric | Imperial |
|---|---|
| 15 g | $\frac{1}{2}$ oz |
| 20 g | $\frac{3}{4}$ oz |
| 25 g | 1 oz |
| 40 g | $1\frac{1}{2}$ oz |
| 50 g | 2 oz |
| 65 g | $2\frac{1}{2}$ oz |
| 75 g | 3 oz |
| 100 g | $3\frac{1}{2}$ oz |
| 125 g | 4 oz |
| 150 g | 5 oz |
| 175 g | 6 oz |
| 200 g | 7 oz |
| 250 g | 8 oz |
| 275 g | 9 oz |
| 300 g | 10 oz |
| 325 g | 11 oz |
| 350 g | 12 oz |
| 375 g | 13 oz |
| 400 g | 14 oz |
| 425 g | 15 oz |
| 500 g | 1 lb |
| 625 g | $1\frac{1}{4}$ lb |
| 750 g | $1\frac{1}{2}$ lb |
| 875 g | $1\frac{3}{4}$ lb |
| 1 kg | 2 lb |
| 1.25 kg | $2\frac{1}{2}$ lb |
| 1.5 kg | 3 lb |
| 1.75 kg | 4 lb |
| 2 kg | $4\frac{1}{2}$ lb |
| 2.25 kg | 5 lb |

# Liquid Measures

| Metric | Imperial |
|---|---|
| 100 ml | 4 fl oz |
| 150 ml | $\frac{1}{4}$ pt |
| 200 ml | 6 fl oz |
| 300 ml | $\frac{1}{2}$ pt |
| 350 ml | 12 fl oz |
| 400 ml | 14 fl oz |
| 450 ml | $\frac{3}{4}$ pt |
| 500 ml | 18 fl oz |
| 600 ml | 1 pt |
| 750 ml | $1\frac{1}{4}$ pts |
| 900 ml | $1\frac{1}{2}$ pts |
| 1 l | $1\frac{3}{4}$ pts |
| 1.2 l | 2 pts |
| 1.25 l | $2\frac{1}{4}$ pts |
| 1.5 l | $2\frac{1}{2}$ pts |
| 1.75 l | 3 pts |
| 2 l | $3\frac{1}{2}$ pts |
| 2.25 l | 4 pts |
| 2.5 l | $4\frac{1}{2}$ pts |
| 2.75 l | 5 pts |

# Oven Temperatures

| Gas Mark | Centigrade | Fahrenheit |
|---|---|---|
| 1 | 140° | 275° |
| 2 | 150° | 300° |
| 3 | 170° | 325° |
| 4 | 180° | 350° |
| 5 | 190° | 375° |
| 6 | 200° | 400° |
| 7 | 220° | 425° |
| 8 | 230° | 450° |

*Note to American readers: 1 tbsp = 15 ml; 1 pt = $2\frac{1}{2}$ US cups.*
ALL QUANTITIES GIVEN ARE APPROXIMATE.

# Acknowledgements

For permission to quote extracts from copyright works, my thanks to the following: Nigel Nicolson for *The Land* by V. Sackville-West on pp. 40, 86 and 123; Secker & Warburg for the poems of Andrew Young on pp. 77, 90 and 102; and Chatto & Windus and the Hogarth Press for *To the Lighthouse* by Virginia Woolf on p. 74.

Sincere thanks to all my friends who have sampled recipes and not only made constructive comments but also offered ideas of their own. I am grateful to Amy Taylor and Dorothy Stansfield for leading me to the poems of Andrew Young and Edward Thomas. My thanks also to all at Penguin Books who have helped in the putting together of *Seasonal Pleasures*.

# Index

# Index